HIDY OCHIAI'S SELF-DEFENSE FOR KIDS

A GUIDE FOR PARENTS AND TEACHERS

Hidy Ochiai

with

Derek Ochiai, M.D.

CB
CONTEMPORARY BOOKS

Library of Congress Cataloging-in-Publication Data

Ochiai, Hidy.
    Hidy Ochiai's self-defense for kids : a guide for parents
and teachers / Hidy Ochiai with Derek Ochiai.
       p.   cm.
    Includes index.
    ISBN 0-8092-2893-9
    1. Self-defense for children.   I. Ochiai, Derek.   II. Title.
III. Title: Self-defense for kids.
GV1111.4.O35   1998   98-12740
613.6'6—DC21   CIP

Cover design by Scott Rattray
Cover photograph by Stephen J. Appel
Interior design by NK Graphics
Interior photographs by Tony Frontera

Published by Contemporary Books
A division of NTC/Contemporary Publishing Group, Inc.
4255 West Touhy Avenue, Lincolnwood (Chicago), Illinois 60646-1975 U.S.A.
Printed in the United States of America
International Standard Book Number: 0-8092-2893-9

99   00   01   02   03   04   VL   6   5   4   3   2   1

Contents

Preface   v

Introduction   1

1   Stretching and Strengthening Exercises   9

2   Basic Stances   41

3   Basic Techniques   51

4   Falling Methods (Ukemi)   103

5   Situational Self-Defense Techniques   113

Index   215

About the Authors   218

Preface

This book is designed to help parents and teachers instruct children of all ages in basic self-defense and safety awareness. It can be used as a textbook for a self-defense class for children, in which case an instructor can go through each technique in the book with the students. Hands-on instruction by a qualified instructor is most important and effective.

This book can also help parents teach their children self-defense techniques at home. By following the book step by step, parents and children can learn together, for all the techniques are applicable to adults as well.

It is my most sincere hope and prayer that this book will help children who face a dangerous situation protect themselves by applying the mental and physical techniques to "get away, run away, right away." The study of self-defense will benefit even those who never face a dangerous situation, which would be most desirable, of course. The practice of self-defense techniques is a tool to enrich the mind as well as to strengthen the body.

I would like to thank Dr. Judith Dogin, professor of child psychology at Case Western School of Medicine, for her valuable input in the preparation of this book. My thanks also go to Brent Ochiai, Renee Cassard, and all junior students who made themselves available for the demonstration of the techniques in this book. Greg Stone's assistance in working with the manuscript is also much appreciated.

Finally, Derek Ochiai was instrumental in creating this book and I enjoyed working with him. He started his study of martial arts at a very early age and has accomplished a great deal in the field of martial arts, especially in karate tournaments. He has also been instrumental in developing an effective self-defense program for children. I wish Dr. Ochiai continued success in his life, both professional and personal.

Hidy Ochiai

D1127258

Introduction

WHY VIOLENCE?

Violence can be found in many different forms in our society—among individuals, among various groups, among nations, and others. One would think that humanity has enough problems coping with natural disasters such as floods, earthquakes, and tornadoes; yet the magnitude of suffering due to these tragic acts of nature is far outweighed by that caused by human acts of violence. It is quite unfortunate that violence is rampant in our streets, schools, and even our homes.

When faced with confrontation, whether from a street mugger, a classmate, a co-worker or supervisor, or anyone exhibiting a threat with physical force, our primal response is the *fight or flight* reaction. This occurs involuntarily, independent of whether the response is appropriate. However, unlike animals, we can use our intellect and self-control based on discipline to harness this natural energy and put it to work in positive ways. If we say that human beings are superior to all other creatures, we must learn to behave in a more dignified fashion deserving of such a claim. We must learn to act peacefully with constant emphasis on mutual respect and the absolute rejection of violence in any form as a means to resolve problems.

DENYING VIOLENCE

Violence takes a tremendous toll on people, individually as well as collectively, and as inhabitants of this planet we have a moral obligation to try to curb violence. An effective start is at the grass-roots level—through the education of our children. If we teach children early in their lives that violence is counterproductive and unacceptable behavior, that attitude can carry over into their adult lives, beginning a general attitude of non-violence. This has to be accomplished by constant emphasis on self-discipline and self-control to the young so that a positive result can be achieved.

It should be kept in mind, however, that non-violence must be dealt with from two sides. Children of all ages must be repeatedly taught not to act with violence toward others; at the same time, we must always be prepared so that we do not become victims of violence. If we successfully teach the concepts of self-discipline and self-control to children and have them practice these qualities in their daily lives, violent children can become less violent and dangerous. Equally important, when children gain additional confidence and increased safety awareness, they will be less likely to become victims of violence.

It would be ideal if we could shield all children from the violent acts depicted on TV and in movies. But if children do view this violence, they must be cautioned each time they watch that the violence they see is not to be imitated in real life. If they are not properly instructed by parents and educators as to the meaninglessness and absurdity of violence, they are apt to imitate violent acts in their own lives.

Children have a difficult time separating fantasy from reality, and they must be strongly cautioned that violence on TV and in movies is fictitious and that violence is not a way to handle problems. Preteen children are in the phase of development where they for the most part think in concrete terms. Thus, they may have trouble separating self-defense practice from actual situations. We must teach children how important it is to respect other people's safety as well as their own.

The techniques described in this book are all defensive in nature and it is clear to adults that they cannot be used aggressively to hurt anyone. However, when children practice the techniques in this book, it is important to stress to them to only use these techniques for true self-defense, not to abuse or misuse them.

SELF-RESPECT

We must teach children how important it is to develop and maintain self-respect for it is the key to non-violent behavior. Only when one learns to respect oneself can one then learn to respect others. It is vital that children be taught that all people live in a society of which they are a part, and that in acting with violence toward others, they diminish themselves. They must learn how to live with others with mutual respect. We must explain to children in a way they understand that in hurting others through violence, they hurt themselves, because we are all one in the human world.

Self-respect is a powerful tool. It fosters the self-confidence one needs to accomplish meaningful goals. This feeling of self-confidence can open new horizons for the child, from academic and athletic improvement to better interpersonal relationships.

Self-respect is the foundation from which other important character traits evolve. For example, it also helps one to develop self-discipline and self-control, which enable one to behave in a decent and socially acceptable manner. Thus it is clear that the prevention of violence among children can be most effectively accomplished by successfully instilling in them a sense of self-respect.

CONFLICT RESOLUTION

It is natural that conflicts happen among children from time to time. The important thing is to teach children how to solve them without resorting to violence. It is effective to remind children of the differences between human beings and animals. Animals, with no rational capacity or reasoning power, naturally choose physical force to resolve conflicts. But children must learn that human society is based on the rational exchange of ideas, not who can hit harder or who is toughest. It has to be stressed in educating children that human beings are endowed with the capacity to reason and we can learn how to solve problems without violence. Communication to gain understanding of the perspective of others is one of the most effective ways to resolve conflicts peacefully.

DEALING WITH ANGER

We all get angry from time to time in varying degrees and forms, and it is not realistic or effective to try to teach children not to become angry. The important thing is to teach children how to express anger in a nondestructive way. Anger can be expressed in a socially acceptable way by directing one's energy in a constructive manner. Violence is usually committed by children who know no other way to express their anger. An emphasis on self-control and self-discipline is essential in educating children.

POSTURE AND BREATHING

From ancient times martial arts masters have realized the importance of good, strong posture together with quiet, controlled breathing, which can have a tremendous impact on one's mental condition. Simply stated, one's physiological state greatly affects one's psychological condition. It is no accident, then, that martial arts students, taught by an authentic teacher, come to develop sound character, which is expressed as self-respect, mutual respect, self-reliance, self-discipline, and self-control.

Teach this stance to your children. Stand with your feet shoulder-width apart, keeping your back straight and shoulders down and relaxed. Breathe slowly and quietly through your nose, with the feeling that your lower abdominal area is controlling the breathing. As you maintain this stance, be sure to pull your chin in and direct your eyes forward.

The joining of balance and breathing leads one to develop a sense of inner peace, which helps increase self-awareness and self-confidence, leading to self-control. This affords an opportunity to reflect on one's inner self. Reflection on inner self helps one develop self-awareness and importance of self, which is the basis of self-respect. Self-esteem, on the other hand, is the product of one's perception of how others view him or her, and it can be a positive motivational

tool for accomplishment of one's task. However, self-esteem has to be augmented by self-respect in order to be a positive force for self-development. It is not enough to think that one is good or great, for such feeling can come from hearing others comment on how nice one's clothes are, for example. When people applaud one's performance in athletics or artistic work, self-esteem will rise and self-confidence can develop from it. Self-respect comes from inside the self, and it can be the foundation of one's positive behavior at all times. It should be noted that self-respect spontaneously brings out an attitude of respect for others as well, and this is the reason why its development should be the first priority in children's education. As for self-esteem, it will be developed through social interaction with other children as well as through thoughtful guidance by parents and teachers in daily living situations.

SELF-DEFENSE

The denial of violence must include an ability to defend oneself against violent acts. No one should become a victim of violence, and as we declare that violence has no place in human society, we must also be able to cope with violence successfully when this need arises. One of the traditional martial arts creeds teaches us that one should never provoke a violent confrontation. A true martial arts student should never look for trouble. He learns that the first technique of self-defense at the moment of a potentially dangerous situation is to walk away or even run away from the scene, regardless of one's capability to defend oneself. It must be strictly taught that one should use physical techniques only as the last resort, when walking away or running away is not possible any longer.

MENTAL SELF-DEFENSE

Self-defense techniques do not consist wholly of punches, blocks, and kicks. *Mental* self-defense is more important than the ability to defend oneself physically. One must be alert for potential dangers and avoid them. A true martial arts student will acquire this ability for mental self-defense as she develops more self-confidence through the training of martial arts. Self-respect and respect for others will spontaneously dictate that she seek a non-violent alternative in all situations.

There are many examples of mental self-defense. One important example is to avoid "bad kids" and try to befriend "good kids." It is widely known that even good children can make bad mistakes when under the influence of bad peers. Also, one's mental self-defense can be demonstrated by choosing a well-lit street as opposed to a dark shortcut for an evening errand to a nearby grocery shop, for example.

Respect for Parents and Teachers

It is very important that children learn proper respect for parents, teachers, and authority figures in general. Chances for bad behavior are much less when children pay attention to guidance from parents and teachers, who love and care for children. Of course, there are some regrettable cases that caution us not to make too generalized a statement. It is unfortunate that children must be told that there are some bad adults and they have to be careful of them.

Watch Out for Strangers

Children should also be taught that they should not respond to any inviting gestures or words by a stranger. For example, a stranger may come to a child in the streets and ask him for help to find a lost pet, which is an old trick often used by would-be abductors. A dangerous person does not have to be someone a child is unfamiliar with, but can be any adult who intends to take advantage of or harm a child.

Get Away, Run Away, Right Away

A child must be taught to get away from a dangerous situation first of all. She must run away from the situation right away. Curiosity is a strong instinct for small children and is a wonderful asset in certain situations, such as learning. But they must be taught not to heed curiosity with strangers. A child should not become curious to find out what is going on or what will happen if he stays near a potentially dangerous situation. Mental self-defense, which is based on common sense as well as instinctive judgment for safety, is a powerful tool for all children as well as adults.

Don't Become a Victim

Unfortunately, however, there may be situations where mental self-defense alone is not enough; children in danger must execute physical self-defense techniques so that they may not be victims of violent crimes. We must repeatedly teach children to get away from a dangerous situation at any cost and run away immediately.

PHYSICAL SELF-DEFENSE TECHNIQUES

Contrary to a notion held by many, self-defense techniques in their basic forms are not difficult to learn. In a relatively short time, children can learn basic techniques that will enable them to escape from someone's attempt to grab or choke. Basic blocking techniques such as the upper block and downward block are also learned quickly if taught in a correct way. Basic kicking techniques necessary for self-defense situations, such as the front kick and roundhouse kick, are also relatively easy to learn.

MARTIAL ARTS AND SELF-DEFENSE

Traditional martial arts are different from self-defense techniques. Training in traditional martial arts takes a tremendous amount of time, effort, and energy, based on instruction by an authentic teacher. Self-defense techniques are not necessarily derived from traditional martial arts techniques. For example, in a desperate situation, one may strike an attacker's face with a keychain, which is not a part of traditional martial arts techniques but could be an effective way to discourage the aggressor from further violent acts.

Although traditional martial arts include self-defense, some of the techniques practiced in traditional martial arts may not be immediately applicable to everyday self-defense situations. For example, some movements in traditional martial arts require one to defend oneself against an attacker with a six-foot staff. It is obvious that we do not have much opportunity to apply such techniques in modern days. We must understand this distinction between traditional martial arts techniques and the self-defense techniques necessary in today's world.

Traditional martial arts include an aesthetic appreciation of the physical arts, which were originally developed from self-defense fighting situations in ancient times. This is why there are so many abstract and seemingly meaningless movements in some of the traditional martial arts. They are not actually meaningless, but generally they can only be understood with training under an authentic teacher. In addition, one must be willing to spend a great deal of time and effort to master martial arts of any kind.

SELF-DEFENSE TECHNIQUES

As for the difference between violence and acts of self-defense, the former is destructive, while the latter is a necessary act to maintain one's safety. Children must be taught that violence is not good and is not acceptable in a civilized society. They should also be taught, however, that self-defense is important. No one should be harassed or intimidated by the threat of violence at any time or in any place. When you face such a threat, you must use mental self-defense first of all to secure your safety. When absolutely necessary, however, you must defend yourself with any physical techniques that you know with a full fighting spirit.

DEALING WITH A BULLY

Some children silently suffer harassment from a bully at school or on the playground. It is important that children know how to deal with such a situation. For example, what should a child do when someone demands his lunch money at school? What if a bully keeps bothering a child and will not leave him alone? Or, what should a child do when one of her classmates wants to fight her against her will? These are all real situations that can happen anywhere. Some children are just scared and endure humiliation and beatings by bad kids, but there is no reason this has to happen.

We must help children develop an ability to be resourceful so that they can cope with unfortunate situations at school or elsewhere. First of all, we must teach children that there are alternatives to taking abuse from a bully. One of the important ways to solve such problems may be to utilize a system of mediation by authorities such as school officials, counselors, teachers, and principals. Peer mediation can also be effective in many cases. A group of students with leadership ability would meet with victims and perpetrators to openly talk to both sides and let the parties involved talk to each other in a safe atmosphere. This face-to-face peaceful confrontation often proves to be very effective for solving a problem between students.

A student should be encouraged to come up with different tactics that could be ordinary or innovative. At one time she may try to humor the bully, and at another time she may take a firm stand against the bully. It may be helpful to find out something about the bully such as his likes and dislikes—she can then try to carry on a conversation along the line of his interests to calm him down. When violence is about to erupt, she could change the whole course of action by radically changing the focus to a completely different subject. She may simply call out someone's name as though that person were nearby. She may call out the name of a teacher the bully knows. Whatever the means she may choose, she must do all she can to avoid becoming a victim of violence and harassment, including running away.

STANDING UP

In certain situations, a victim may have to stand up to a bully or anyone who keeps bothering him. He may have to come up with some tactics to solve a problem by himself. After all other conflict resolution methods fail, the victim may finally have to say to the bully "Hey, I am not afraid of you, but I don't want to fight you because I hate violence. I have too much self-respect to engage in violence as cats and dogs do. I want to know what can stop you from

bothering me." From this point, the two can interact as individuals with feelings and needs. They may be able to develop conversations by using different topics such as movies, books, sports, and so on. Incidentally, this is an application of the highest stage of martial strategy—resolving a conflict without fighting.

This sudden resolute attitude of the victim will change the bully's perception and weaken his aggression, for it involves diverting his attention and negative energy. This is a powerful weapon as well.

DETEST VIOLENCE

A violent individual is similar to an aggressive animal. If one appears timid and fearful of him, that person will become a more attractive target of his violent behavior. It is important that she show no fear—in her eyes she must show that she detests violence but is not afraid of it. When she is successful demonstrating her confidence and inner strength, a bully or violent individual often backs away. Through the study of self-defense techniques and mental self-defense in this book, a child will eventually come to develop such self-confidence, which in turn will help her to become a truly non-violent person: not acting with violence toward anyone, yet at the same time not becoming a victim of violence.

A STRONG PERSON

There is a natural tendency among some children to discuss who is the toughest. It is vital that adults discuss with children the meaning of strength in a person. The unfortunate thing is that the children have a tendency to believe that anyone who can fight well physically is a

How to Teach Kids to Practice Among Kids

Teach them . . .

- To practice each technique with a serious attitude. No fooling around should be allowed during the practice of self-defense techniques lest children injure themselves or their partners.
- To always keep two things in mind: (1) they must practice each technique in slow motion in the beginning for the sake of safety as well as better understanding, and (2) they must follow each technique in a correct manner. Remember that an incorrectly executed technique may not work. Have them go back to the demonstrations and explanations of each technique repeatedly to learn correct technique.
- To learn the self-defense techniques but not abuse them. The best self-defense is mental self-defense, by which they protect themselves without having to resort to physical techniques.
- To develop confidence through serious and repetitive practice of the techniques described in this book.
- To execute self-respect and mutual respect at all times during practice as well as daily life. Teach them that self-discipline is the basis for acquiring self-control, confidence, concentration, and willpower.

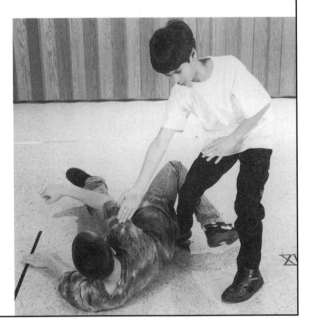

strong person. Children must be taught that a truly strong person is one who has self-control, self-respect, and self-confidence, and who is not eager to control others but knows how to maintain self-control at all times.

Violence should not be glorified in any way. Respect from others cannot be demanded or taken, but can only be earned by responsible behavior. When this definition of personal strength is taught to children all the time, schoolyard fights may occur less and less as the absurdity of violence becomes clear to them.

1 Stretching and Strengthening Exercises

For the purpose of self-defense training, as distinguished from traditional martial arts training, it is not really necessary to go through vigorous physical exercises. It is important, however, that you start warm-up exercises gently and end your workout with similar gentle movements. Never start with an exercise that requires a hard muscle movement or cardiovascular stress.

Perform each warm-up exercise at least a few times. The level of your training workout may require more repetitions. Listen to your body and adjust your warm-up routine as needed.

A minimum amount of warming up is required for the sake of preventing injury during the practice of the techniques. If your body is loose and flexible, you can execute a technique in a more efficient way and decrease the chance of pulling muscles or otherwise injuring yourself. In order to further prevent injury, remember to always perform exercises at your own pace—don't feel pressured to go too fast.

BREATHE IN–BREATHE OUT EXERCISE

1. Start with this simple breathe in–breathe out exercise. Inhale slowly by pulling your diaphragm downward.

2. Exhale by pushing your stomach in and pushing your diaphragm upward. At the start of warm-up exercises, perform this exaggerated breathing twice; at the conclusion of the warm-up period, perform this breathing exercise three times.

UPPER-BODY ROTATION

1. Open your feet wide and start to rotate your upper body from the bending-forward position.

2. Try to bend your upper body fully sideward as you keep both of your arms extended.

3. Bend your upper body backward as well.

4. This exercise should be performed in a slow, gentle motion in the beginning. Rotate your upper body from right to left and then left to right.

BASIC STRETCHES

1. Stand with your feet wide apart, both feet flat on the floor. Place your weight gently on the left foot by bending the left knee as shown. The right knee is straight with the right foot flat on the floor.

2. Place your weight gently on the right foot by bending the right knee as shown. Keep the left foot flat on the floor and stretch the left knee. Repeat the exercise on both sides.

1. Keep your feet open wide and bend the left knee with the left foot flat on the floor. Stretch the right knee and let the right foot stand with its heel on the floor. Bend your upper body comfortably forward as shown.

2. Bend your right knee and straighten the left knee. Keep the right foot flat on the floor and let the left foot stand on its heel on the floor.

1. Turn your left foot to the left and place about 70 percent of your weight on it by bending the left knee. Both feet are flat on the floor. Push your upper body to the left to feel the weight and force on the left leg.

2. Turn your right foot to the right and place about 70 percent of your weight on it by bending the right knee. Both feet are flat on the floor. Push your upper body to the right to feel the weight and force on the right leg.

1. Sit on the floor with your right knee bent. Keep the left knee straight.

2. Bring your head forward gradually as you breathe out. Push your head forward until it touches the floor. Hold this position for a few seconds.

3. Sit on the floor with your left knee bent. Keep the right knee straight.

4. Bring your head forward gradually as you breathe out. Push your head forward until it touches the floor. Again, hold this position for a few seconds.

1. Sit on the floor with your legs open as wide as possible as shown here. Keep your knees straight.

2. As you exhale slowly, bend forward until your head touches the floor. Hold this final position for a few seconds.

1. Starting in a wide stance, bend your right knee completely, keeping your left knee straight. Keep your left foot on its heel. Lean forward slightly and press the left leg on the floor. Do not sit down.

2. Bend your left knee completely, keeping your right knee straight. Keep your right foot on its heel. Lean forward slightly and press the right leg on the floor. Do not sit. Perform this exercise and all others at your own pace.

1. From a sitting position, open your legs as wide as possible and keep both knees straight. As you exhale, push your upper body and head to the left leg slowly, and hold the position for a few seconds.

2. Push your upper body and head to the right leg slowly, and hold the position for a few seconds. Remember to perform this exercise and all others at your own pace.

1. Stretch both legs linearly—as when doing the splits—facing your right. Try to keep both knees as straight as possible. Bring your upper body and head to the right leg, and hold this final posture for a few seconds.

2. Bring your upper body and head to the left leg, and hold this position for a few seconds. Remember to perform this exercise and all others at your own pace.

ARM EXERCISES

1. Stand with feet shoulder-width apart. Extend your arms in front of you.

2. Stretch your arms to the side.

3. Bring your arms again in front of you.

4. Pull back both arms to your sides, assuming the position shown. Repeat the whole motion several times.

NECK EXERCISE

1. Stand straight with your feet shoulder-width apart. Relax your shoulders. Close your eyes for a couple of seconds before you start moving your neck.

2. Bend your neck sideward gently and hold the position for a couple of seconds. Repeat on the other side.

3. Tuck your chin down as if to look down at your feet. Hold this position for a couple of seconds.

4. Look up slightly, moving slowly, and hold this position for a few seconds. You may also loosen your neck by gently rotating it clockwise and counterclockwise. Do *not* tilt your head backwards dramatically, as doing so can cause damage to your neck or spine.

PUSH-UPS

1. This is the standard push-up. Begin in the position shown, with arms extended and shoulder-width apart, palms on the floor. Bend your elbows and lower your upper body toward the floor until your elbows are bent at a 90-degree angle.

2. Concentrating the effort in your arms, push your body back up to the starting position. Keep your feet together and feel your weight on your hands each time as you bend and stretch your arms.

1. Push-ups on knuckles.

2. You may perform this push-up by placing your knuckles so that the palm sides face each other as well.

1. Push-ups on knees.

2. Those who find it difficult to perform regular push-ups may start with this method. This is still effective in strengthening your arms.

1. Push-ups on fingers.

2. Do not perform this exercise too rapidly.

1. Push-ups with one hand.

2. This push-up is not for everyone. Use your own discretion in attempting it. Place the other hand on your back.

LEG EXERCISES

1. Lie on the floor on your back and kick out each foot in turn.

2. Push the heel of each foot out. Perform this exercise with varying speed and power—slow and strong, fast and light, and so on.

1. Lie on your right side and support yourself with your right arm and elbow.

2. Kick your left foot out straight sideward. Imagine that you are executing a side kick. Repeat this exercise with the right leg as well.

1. Lie down on your right side, supporting yourself with your right elbow and arm. Tuck in your left knee and prepare to kick.

2. Kick upward with the outer edge of your left foot. Try to feel an execution of the high side kick. Repeat this exercise with the right leg as well.

1. Get on the floor on both hands and feet. Raise your hips high with legs straight.

2. Bring your leg back high, keeping its knee straight. Repeat the exercise on the other leg.

ABDOMINAL EXERCISES

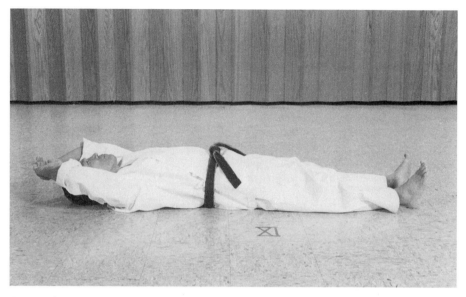

1. Lie down on your back as shown.

2. Bring your upper body up without moving your feet off the floor or bending your knees. Repeat this exercise at your own pace.

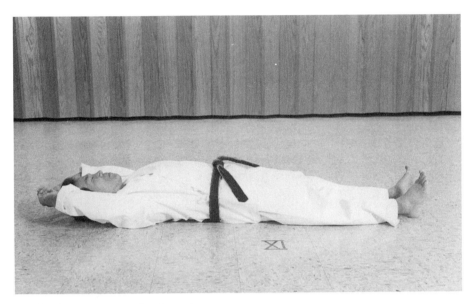

1. Lie down on your back as shown.

2. Inhale deeply and, as you exhale, bring your upper body and legs slowly up and hold this position for several seconds. Return to the original position and relax for a couple of seconds before repeating the motion.

1. Get on the floor on your knees. Inhale and exhale deeply a couple of times.

2. After you exhale, bend your upper body backward gently as you inhale until your head touches the floor. Remember to perform this exercise at your own pace. (You don't have to touch your head on the floor, but go back as far as you can.)

CARDIOVASCULAR EXERCISES

1. Get on the floor with both hands and feet. Bring one foot forward as if you were preparing to sprint. Switch your feet rapidly.

2. Try to bring your front foot as far forward as possible. Move your feet quickly for a minute or two to get a good cardiovascular workout. Remember to perform this exercise at your own pace.

1. Get on the floor on both hands and feet. Extend both legs.

2. Bring both feet together forward and then push them back to the original position. Repeat the motion at a rapid pace for a cardiovascular exercise.

KNEE EXERCISES

1. Place your feet and knees together and bend the knees fully. Grab your knees with both hands.

2. Rotate your knees from right to left and left to right.

3. Keep your feet flat on the floor.

1. Stand as in the front stance (see page 46), placing more weight on your front leg. Your back leg is straight, but not tense.

2. Bring your back leg forward by bending its knee fully to touch the chest.

3. Bring your foot back to its original position. Repeat on the other leg as well. Repeat the whole motion as many times as you wish according to your own pace.

2 Basic Stances

Stances are the most important part of learning the techniques. A good, proper stance will enable you to maintain good balance, which is necessary to make it possible for you to execute a good technique. A good stance is also connected to a good mental condition. We must constantly remember that mind and body are connected. A strong, stable stance is a manifestation of a strong, confident mind.

ATTENTION STANCE

Keep your back straight with your shoulders relaxed and eyes focused on one point. Pull your chin in and keep your mouth closed with quiet breathing through the nose. Stand with a feeling of pushing your stomach slightly outward. Keep the knees straight but not tight. Keep your feet together with heels touching and both feet open to 45 degrees.

This stance is conducive to a sense of self-respect. When you bow to your partner from this stance, you are symbolically showing respect for others, not only your immediate partner. When one attains self-respect, she can respect others.

NATURAL STANCE

Open your feet to shoulder width with the toes pointing outward. Keep your back straight and shoulders relaxed. Try to breathe quietly through your nose by feeling power in the lower abdomen. Focus your eyes on one spot, but be aware of the surroundings.

This stance is connected with your mental focus, readiness, and concentration. Self-discipline is essential as you form this stance.

FRONT STANCE

Open your feet shoulder-width apart and two natural footsteps in length, with one foot in front of the other. About 60 percent of the weight should be distributed on the front leg, while the remaining 40 percent should be on the back leg. Point your front foot straight ahead and your back foot outward at a 45-degree angle to the front foot. Keep your back straight and push your stomach outward with a feeling of power in the lower abdomen.

You gain a feeling of physical stability from this stance, and that will encourage your sense of self-confidence. As you proceed forward with this stance, maintaining the center of your gravity at a constant level, you will feel self-assuredness and self-confidence that can be applied in any setting in a positive manner.

HALF-AND-HALF STANCE

Place your feet at the same width and length as in the front stance, but distribute your weight evenly over both legs. The front foot faces about the same direction as the back foot. Knees are bent and relaxed so that you can change to the front stance if needed at any time.

This stance emphasizes the concept of self-control. You must show that you are truly a strong person because you do not act on impulse and you know how to control yourself.

ATTENTION STANCE

Stand with your heels together and toes pointed about 45 degrees outward. Keep your shoulders down and relaxed and try to feel quiet power in your lower stomach. Breathe quietly and slowly through your nose. Focus your eyes on one spot but maintain awareness of your surroundings. This is the stance that demonstrates your sense of self-respect, without which you cannot respect others.

MUTUAL BOW

1. In the practice of self-defense, you must show proper respect to your partner. It is a mutual respect. Although in a real situation you are defending yourself against an opponent, in practice it is a partner who helps you make progress in the art of self-defense. Face each other in the attention stance.

2. Bend slowly from the waist and direct your eyes downward. Lift your head and raise your upper body back to its original position. The mutual bow is an important gesture because it distinguishes your action from violence and demonstrates respect. It also reminds you that you are practicing tools for non-violence, not for violence.

NATURAL STANCE

1. Open your feet sideways to one shoulder width. Stand with a relaxed feeling and your eyes focused. Your shoulders are down and relaxed, and you should feel a quiet power from your lower abdominal area.

2. Breathe slowly and quietly. Do not pull your stomach in.

FRONT STANCE

1. Step forward so that your front foot is two natural steps in front of your back foot. Keep your feet about one shoulder-width apart. Bend your front knee so that it is right over your instep. Distribute about 60 percent of your weight over the front foot, and 40 percent over the back foot.

2. Keep your shoulders down and relaxed. Keep your back straight, maintaining a feeling of pushing your stomach outward a little. In this stance, you demonstrate a sense of self-confidence. The stable, comfortable stance gives you a mental stability that connects with your sense of self-confidence.

HALF-AND-HALF STANCE

1. This is a ready-to-defend posture. Although you detest violence and do everything possible to avoid any violent confrontation, if you are in danger and cannot simply run away, you must defend yourself by facing your opponent with confidence, concentration, and full fighting spirit.

2. Squat down with equal weight placed on each leg and be prepared to move in any direction. Your eyes should be focused on the opponent. Keep your back straight and shoulders down and relaxed. Practice various defensive and offensive techniques from this stance.

APPLIED STANCES

Front Stance with Downward Block

Keep your shoulders relaxed and back straight with power in the stomach. Your blocking arm is about parallel to the line of your front thigh. Demonstrate a sense of self-confidence.

Front Stance with Lunge Punch

Push your back foot flat against the floor and bend your front knee in such a way that it is perpendicular to the floor or the knee drops over the instep.

Front-Stance Attack and Defending from the Natural Stance

The attacker is ready to execute a technique from the front stance. The defender is ready to react from the natural stance.

Blocking a Kick from the Half-and-Half Stance

The defender uses the half-and-half stance as he blocks the partner's front kick.

Blocking a Punch from the Half-and-Half Stance

The defender uses the half-and-half stance as he blocks the partner's middle attack with the inside-outward block.

Blocking a Punch from the Half-and-Half Using the Outside-Inward Block

The defender executes the outside-inward block by assuming the half-and-half stance.

3   Basic Techniques

Since this is a book on self-defense and not karate per se, the basic techniques included here are limited. However, if learned well, they are sufficient in most self-defense situations. Proper understanding of the techniques and repeated practice with patience are needed to acquire mastery. It should be emphasized again that instruction from a qualified teacher of martial arts is most beneficial to anyone who wishes to become proficient in the art of self-defense.

The techniques covered in this chapter are

- Making a fist
- Punching
- Blocks (upper, downward, inside-outward, outside-inward)
- Punch and block combinations
- Elbow strikes (front, upper, side, back, downward)
- Kicks (front, side, roundhouse, back)
- Roundhouse knee kick

MAKING A FIST (A)

1. Open your hand to prepare to make a fist.

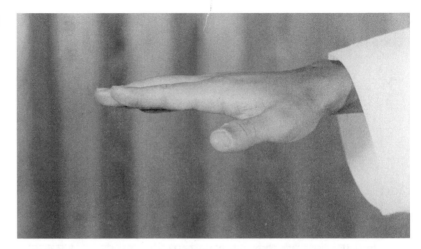

2. Bend the first and the second joints of your four fingers.

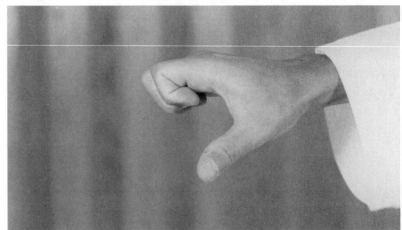

3. Curl your fingertips into your palm.

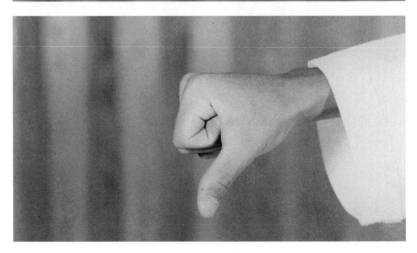

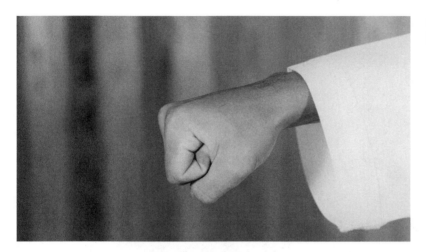

4. Bend your thumb to cover your index finger.

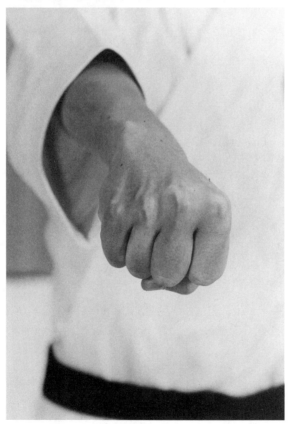

5. The fist should be securely formed, but it should not be tight. At the moment of the execution of the punch, the fist tightens and immediately relaxes.

MAKING A FIST (B)

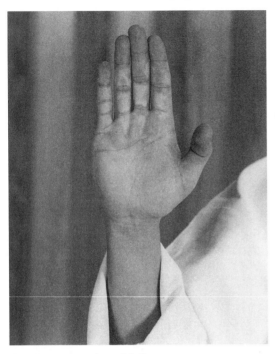

1. Open your hand fully.

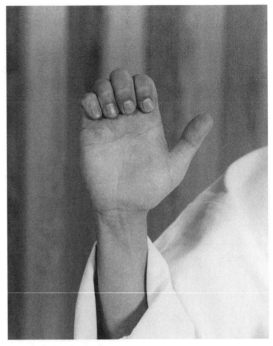

2. Bend your fingers in such a way that their tips touch the top of your palm.

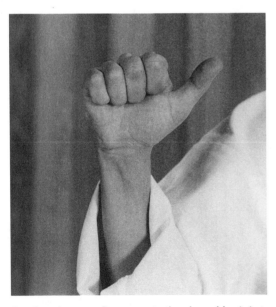

3. Bend your fingers at the knuckle joints tightly. Make sure that your little finger does not become weak.

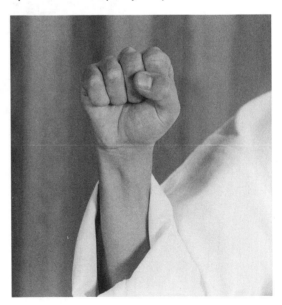

4. Now bend your thumb and tuck it tightly over your index finger.

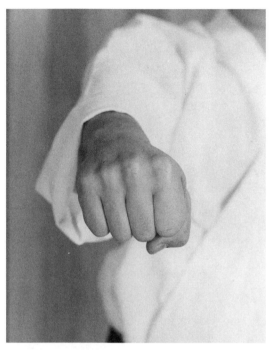

5. The point of contact on the target consists mainly of the first two knuckles. Keep the back of the wrist straight.

PUNCHING (A)

1. Place your punching hand just above the hip bone with its palm side facing upward. Extend your other hand straight in front.

2. Now simultaneously begin to push your punching hand out and to pull your other hand toward your hip. The pulling hand is important because the basic principle of action-reaction is applied in the execution of punching.

3. As you throw your punching hand out, make sure that its elbow rubs the side of your body, thus ensuring that your punching hand travels the shortest distance possible to the target by following a straight line. After the elbow passes your body, begin to rotate your wrist inward until your palm faces the floor. Do not rotate your wrist too early!

4. Keep your shoulders relaxed throughout the punching motion. Synchronize your punching arm (throwing out) and your pulling hand (retracting).

PUNCHING (B)

1. Extend your pulling hand (the right hand in the photo) straight in line with the middle of your chest. (The point straight in front of your own solar plexus can be a good target as well.) Hold your punching hand just above the hip bone.

2. As you start to throw your punching hand out, be careful not to let its elbow come off your body.

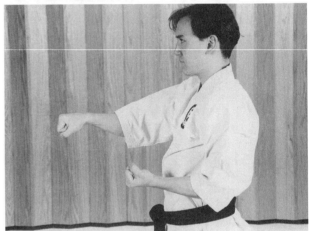

3. Don't twist your punching fist until its elbow completely passes the body. The elbow of the punching arm causes friction against the body until it passes beyond it.

4. Keep your shoulders low and relaxed so that the punching hand can travel quickly and effectively.

5. Maintain power in the lower abdominal area as you execute the punching technique. It is important to synchronize the punching hand and the pulling hand.

UPPER BLOCK

1. Assuming the natural stance, bring your right (pulling) arm above your forehead in a blocking motion. In this preparatory posture, your right hand is open as shown here.

2. Bring your left (blocking) arm up as you slide it out from the side of the hip. Your left fist should be directed toward your right shoulder with its elbow kept low. Begin to lower your pulling arm.

3. The blocking (left) arm crosses outside of the pulling arm, meeting in front of the neck. Observe that the blocking arm is not twisted yet, and its elbow is not raised yet.

4. At the completion of the upper block, the left arm is twisted in such a way that the palm side faces the opponent. The elbow of the blocking arm should be bent approximately 120 degrees and it should be about one to one and a half fists in distance from the forehead. The pulling arm returns to a relaxed, cocked position at the right hip.

5. You block your opponent's left upper lunge punch with your left arm by stepping back with your right foot to assume the front stance.

6. You block your opponent's right upper lunge punch with your right arm by stepping back with your left foot to assume the half-and-half stance.

DOWNWARD BLOCK

1. Bring the pinkie side of your right fist to the joint between the left shoulder and the arm.

2. Slide your right fist down along the left arm. Do not twist your right fist until its elbow becomes extended.

3. At the completion of the block, your right palm is facing downward and your left fist is pulled to the side of the hip.

4. Let's take a look at the downward block from another angle. Bring your left fist to your right shoulder. (Your left palm faces your right cheek.)

5. Slide your left fist down along your right arm without any twisting motion.

6. Twist your left fist in such a way that its palm faces downward at the moment of blocking. Pull back your right fist to the side of the hip.

7. As you receive your partner's front kick, execute the right-arm downward block by stepping back with your left foot to assume the half-and-half stance or the front stance.

INSIDE-OUTWARD BLOCK

1. Cross your arms fully with palms downward. The blocking arm (the right arm in this case) is placed underneath the pulling arm.

2. Move your right forearm in an arc toward the right, pivoting at the elbow. In the same way, move your left arm in an arc toward your left hip.

3. At the completion of the block, your right palm faces toward you with the fist at shoulder level. Your left arm has been pulled to the side and rests near the left hip bone, palm up.

4. Let's look at the block from the side. Cross your arms as shown with the left arm underneath the right. (The left arm is the blocking arm in this case.)

5. Move your left fist counterclockwise with its elbow as the pivot point, while you pull your right fist toward the hip.

6. Your left fist ends up at shoulder level with its palm facing toward you. Your right fist rests near the right hip bone, palm up.

7. Your partner executes the right middle lunge punch, which you block with the right inside-outward block as you step back with your left foot and assume the half-and-half stance.

OUTSIDE-INWARD BLOCK

1. Bring your blocking (right) arm to shoulder height with the palm facing downward. The pulling arm is extended straight in front.

2. Bring your right fist toward the midsection of the body. Do not twist your fist until the moment of execution of the block. Bend your left elbow and begin to pull it back toward the left hip.

3. At the moment of the block, your right elbow is lowered. Your fist is stabilized at shoulder level with the palm facing upward. Your left wrist rests near the left hip bone.

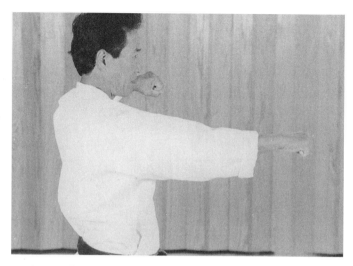

4. Let's look at this block from another angle. Extend your right arm straight in front of you for the ready-to-pull position. Raise your blocking arm to shoulder level with its palm facing downward.

5. At the completion of the block, the elbow of your blocking arm should not be too far away from your body, about one to one and a half fists.

6. In application of the outside-inward block, it is natural that the angle of the elbow could change.

7. This block could also be applied with an up-and-down motion against the opponent's middle attack.

PUNCH AND BLOCK COMBINATIONS

Upper Block and Basic Punch

1. Your partner executes a right upper punch, which you block with your left arm using the upper block technique.

2. Grab your partner's attacking arm with your blocking arm and counterattack with your right upper punch.

Outside-Inward Block and Backfist Strike

1. Your partner executes a right middle punch, which you block with a right middle outside-inward block.

2. Grab the attacking arm with your left hand.

3. Execute a backfist strike to your partner's face at the philtrum (the point below the nose). The backfist strike can be executed in one of two ways: snapping or thrusting. In a snapping backfist strike, you will snap the elbow to reach the target in arc, while in a thrusting backfist strike, you will thrust out the fist straight to the target in the shortest distance. Make sure that there is no contact in practice.

FRONT ELBOW STRIKE

1. Your partner executes an upper lunge attack, which you block with your right arm while stepping back with your left foot and assuming the half-and-half stance.

2. Press down your partner's attacking arm with your left open hand by pulling back your right foot slightly and pivoting your body to the right.

3. Step forward with your foot to the outside of your partner's right foot to prepare for execution of the front elbow strike.

4. Use your right elbow to strike your partner's right midsection. Depending on how you set yourself up in relation to your opponent, the elbow strike can be executed to the solar plexus, the ribcage, or the temple.

UPPER ELBOW STRIKE

1. From the natural stance, block your partner's right upper lunge punch.

2. Grab your partner's attacking arm with your blocking arm. Step in with the right foot as you prepare for the upper elbow strike.

3. Bring your partner's attacking arm close to your body as you execute the upper elbow strike, hitting your partner's jaw with your elbow. Be sure to avoid contact in practice. Move your right arm in an upward motion. The palm of your striking arm should face your right temple at the completion of the technique, with your fist near your ear.

4. The upper elbow strike can be executed to the opponent's midsection (solar plexus) as well.

SIDE ELBOW STRIKE

1. Assuming the natural stance, block your partner's upper attack from your right side.

2. Grab the attacking arm with your left hand.

3. Bring your right arm across your midsection with its fist showing its palm side upward.

4. Slide closer to the target with your right foot to execute the side elbow strike. Observe that your right palm faces downward at the completion of the technique.

BACK ELBOW STRIKE

1. Assuming the natural stance, you are being choked by your partner with a one-arm choke.

2. Bring your left arm straight forward with its fist showing its palm side downward.

3. Execute the back elbow strike to your partner's midsection by pulling back strongly your left arm in such a way that the palm faces upward at the completion of the technique.

DOWNWARD ELBOW STRIKE

1. You face your partner with a ready-to-defend stance.

2. Your partner lunges forward with an attempt to tackle you. Stop your partner's lunge motion by pressing his head down and pulling toward you with your open hand.

3. Step back with your right foot as you take your partner down to the floor by pulling him forward.

4. Be ready to counterattack with the downward elbow strike. Raise your right arm high with its fist showing its palm side away from you.

5. Execute the strike to the bottom of your partner's skull. Your right knee touches the floor as you execute the technique. Make sure that your downward elbow strike is executed in such a way that your fist is twisted at the completion of the technique to show its palm side toward you. In practice, it is essential to avoid contact.

FRONT KICK (METHOD A)

1. Your partner executes an upper punch with the minor front stance (one-step forward stance). Block with your right arm from the natural stance. Hold your left arm up as in the beginning of the ready-to-defend posture.

2. Grab your partner's attacking arm with both your hands as you pull it down to break your partner's balance.

3. Bring your right foot to the level of your left knee. Keep holding your partner's right arm as you prepare the front kick.

4. Execute the kick to your partner's midsection. Make sure that the ball of your kicking foot (the right foot in this case) is directed to the target. In the beginning, it is good to practice in slow motion and gradually increase speed. Make sure that you do not make any contact with your partner's body while practicing.

FRONT KICK (METHOD B)

1. Block your partner's upper punch with your right arm by stepping back with your left foot to assume a high half-and-half stance.

2. Grab your partner's attacking arm with your left hand and pull it forward to break the partner's balance. Slide your right foot back to adjust the distance for the kick.

3. Execute a high front kick to your partner's chin (without any contact in practice). The supporting foot must be stable for a good kick. In an actual self-defense situation, it is highly unlikely that one would use such a high front kick, but it is good for practice.

FRONT KICK (METHOD C)

1. As your partner executes the right lunge punch, you block it with your right arm. Grab your partner's attacking arm with both of your hands. Pull back your right foot slightly to adjust the distance for the kick as above.

2. Execute the left front kick to your partner's midsection as you keep holding your partner's attacking arm.

SIDE KICK (METHOD A)

1. In solo practice, concentrate on an imaginary opponent and target area.

2. Bring the kicking foot high with the supporting foot facing the same direction as the kicking foot.

3. Execute a side kick to the midsection of your imaginary opponent. Let the kicking foot show its edge to the target with its toes curled up.

In the snap side kick, the kicking foot travels in a slight arc, while in the thrust side kick it travels the shortest distance possible (straight line) to the target.

4. A high side kick is usually directed to an opponent's chin or throat.

5. Good balance is essential for any kick.

SIDE KICK (METHOD B)

1. Your partner executes a right upper lunge punch, which you block with your left arm by stepping back with your right foot.

2. Grab your partner's right arm with your left hand as you bring your right hand to temple level. Adjust the supporting foot (the right foot in this case) to the correct distance for the kick.

3. Execute the left side kick to your partner's midsection. The supporting foot must be stable for an effective kick. In practice, one must be careful not to make any contact with the partner's body.

4. A high side kick is usually directed to the opponent's chin or throat. In this case, the snap side kick is more often used than the thrust side kick.

5. In an actual self-defense situation, a low side kick (thrust) to the opponent's knee, shin, or groin area can be effective to offset the opponent's aggression.

SIDE KICK (METHOD C)

1. Block your partner's upper punch with your left arm by stepping back with your right foot.

2. Grab your partner's attacking arm with your left hand and pull it down to offset your partner's balance. Adjust the supporting foot for the correct distance for the kick.

3. In preparation for the kick, you must bring your kicking foot high with its toes curled upward.

4. In execution of the side kick, your balance must be stable and can be helped by holding onto your partner's arm in practice. A clear distinction must be made between a snap kick and a thrust kick.

ROUNDHOUSE KICK (METHOD A)

1. Your partner executes the right upper punch by taking one step forward (a minor front stance). You block it with your right arm from the natural stance position.

2. Grab your partner's attacking arm with your right hand and pull it down to break your partner's balance.

3. Bring your kicking knee and foot high with its toes curled up in preparation for the kick.

4. Execute the kick to your partner's solar plexus area by throwing the kicking foot as you would throw your arm. The supporting foot turns about 90 degrees in the direction of the kick to accommodate the roundhouse movement of the kick.

In practice, there should not be any contact with your partner's body. In a real self-defense situation, this kick can be directed to the lower part of the opponent's body.

ROUNDHOUSE KICK (METHOD B)

1. Your partner executes the right upper lunge punch, which you block with your right arm by stepping back with your left foot to assume the half-and-half stance. Grab the attacking arm with your right hand.

2. Bring your left foot slightly forward to adjust the distance for the kick. Keep holding your partner's attacking arm to keep your partner off-balance.

3. Execute the right roundhouse kick to your partner's midsection (solar plexus). The supporting foot (the left foot in this case) turns about 90 degrees at the same time as the roundhouse kick is executed.

4. A high roundhouse kick is usually directed to the opponent's temple. In practice, you must be careful not to make any contact with your partner's body.

5. Let's look at the roundhouse kick to your partner's midsection from another angle. Your balance at the moment of kicking is very important.

6. Here is another look at the high roundhouse kick to your partner's temple. The stability of the supporting foot is essential for a good, powerful kick.

BACK KICK (METHOD A)

1. You block your partner's right upper lunge punch with your left arm by stepping back with your right foot to assume the half-and-half stance.

2. As you turn your back to your partner, adjust your supporting foot for the correct distance for the back kick with your left foot.

3. Your kicking foot must be raised high as you look over your shoulder to the target. Your supporting foot is pointing away from the target.

4. At the moment you kick, the toes of the kicking foot should be facing downward. The point of contact is the heel and its target is the solar plexus in this photo.

BACK KICK (METHOD B)

1. You block your partner's right upper punch with your right arm by stepping back with your left foot.

2. Pull your right foot back closer to your left foot by spinning clockwise. Your right foot now becomes the supporting foot.

3. Raise the kicking foot (the left foot in this case) as you look over the left shoulder to the target.

4. Depending on the angle of your partner's body, you may execute the kick to your partner's floating rib or solar plexus. Shown here is a back kick to the partner's rib area. Strictly observe the no-contact rule in practice.

ROUNDHOUSE KNEE KICK

1. Your partner executes an upper lunge punch, which you block with your right arm by stepping back with your left foot.

2. Grab the attacking arm with your blocking arm. Pull your partner forward with your right hand to break his balance.

3. Bend your right knee completely and bring it high to be ready for the kick.

4. At the moment of execution of the technique, your supporting foot should rotate about 90 degrees to maximize the balance and power of the kick.

4   Falling Methods (Ukemi)

Falling correctly will help you protect yourself when you are thrown on the ground or fall down by accident. All throwing and takedown techniques should only be practiced by those who are familiar with falling methods. It is also true that when you know how to take a fall properly, you will be more confident in performing other techniques because you won't be afraid of falling down.

The most important thing to keep in mind in any falling method is that you should never hit your head on the ground at the moment of the fall. Keep your head up away from the ground and tuck your chin tightly. Make yourself as small as possible, like a ball, absorbing the shock of the impact of falling by hitting your arms on the ground.

SIDE FALL

1. From the sitting position with both legs extended, bring your left arm high with your open hand showing its palm side away from you.

2. As you fall sideways, hit the mat with your open hand and whole arm. Place your weight on the left arm as much as possible with the sensation of making your body small. Bend your knees and keep your head up with chin tucked in.

3. You may practice the side fall from a standing position as well. From the natural stance, move your right foot to the front of your left foot, simultaneously bringing your right arm high above your left shoulder.

4. Practice this technique gently and slowly in the beginning.

5. The important thing is to keep your head up and tuck your chin in. Your hitting arm should be about 45 degrees apart from your body and should support your weight as much as possible.

FRONT FALL

2. The first few times you try this, take the front fall as shown here with your knees touching the ground. Your body is supported by your forearms and your knees.

1. From the kneeling position, bring both arms in front of your face with palms facing away from you.

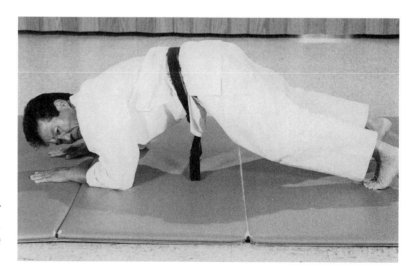

3. The next step is to bring your knees up at the moment of falling. Your face turns to the side at the completion of the fall.

4. Eventually, you may practice the front fall from a standing position. From the natural stance, prepare to fall to the front.

5. Pull back both feet and bring your body forward, simultaneously executing the front fall with both forearms. Make sure that you do not hit your knees at the moment of falling. The hips should be raised up a little at the completion of the fall.

BACK FALL

1. Sit on the mat with both legs extended but relaxed. Cross your arms with the open palms facing downward.

2. As you fall back, bring your arms high and keep your chin tucked in.

3. As you complete the back fall, keep your head up by keeping your chin tightly tucked in. Your arms are about 45 degrees apart from your body. The main idea is to absorb the shock of falling back by hitting the mat strongly with your open hands and arms.

4. You may practice the back fall from the position of squatting down on the balls of your feet as well.

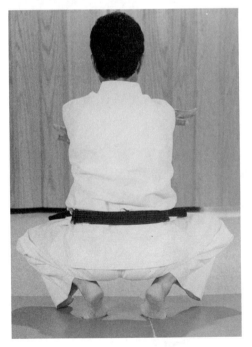

5. As you fall back, bring your arms high and get ready to hit the mat.

6. As you complete the fall, make sure that you keep your chin tucked in so that you never hit your head on the mat.

FRONT ROLLING FALL

1. From the natural stance, take one step forward with your right foot.

2. Place your left hand at the point directly below your left shoulder and in front of your left foot. Bring your right open hand inside your left hand with its outer edge touching the mat.

3. As you start making a roll, maintain the sensation of going over your right arm's outer line to your right shoulder, as if your arms formed an imaginary wheel.

4. Your head does not make any contact with the ground.

5. As you complete the roll, execute the left arm side fall. Again, keep your head up and chin tucked in. The next step is to get up on your feet as you finish the fall, using your rolling momentum to propel you.

5

Situational
Self-Defense Techniques

Children must learn each situational self-defense technique step by step with patience. They must be constantly reminded of the difference between violence and self-defense: violence is detrimental and hurtful, whereas self-defense is necessary for children's safety. Practicing self-defense techniques can be a lot of fun, as well as challenging. The techniques must be executed properly in a controlled and systematic manner. Therefore, it is crucial that parents and teachers familiarize themselves with the techniques so they can effectively help their children learn them.

MENTAL SELF-DEFENSE

Situations that call for self-defense techniques are infinite in variety. Many of those situations can be handled with mental self-defense techniques as explained earlier in this book (page 4). Common sense and instinctive judgment are very important in mental self-defense. And in most cases we can protect ourselves without engaging in physical self-defense.

Children should be taught, therefore, that they must be aware of strangers, bad people, belligerent peers, and any person who might harm them. They must learn to walk or run away at once from any potential danger. Teach children to "think safe, be safe."

TECHNIQUES TO GET AWAY, RUN AWAY, RIGHT AWAY

Unfortunately, however, mental self-defense techniques alone may not be enough for every situation. For example, someone grabs a child's hand before the child can escape. Or someone grabs a child by the neck from behind when the child is not prepared. In these cases a child must act with all his physical strength and techniques he knows to free himself from an assailant. In an emergency situation, there is no distinction between mental self-defense and physical self-defense; one's only obligation is to protect oneself from danger.

PRACTICE WITH PATIENCE

Although possible situations that require physical self-defense techniques are infinite in number, it is only through a limited number of prearranged forms that we can teach children how to protect themselves. Through the repeated practice of prearranged techniques, children develop skill, understanding, and confidence that they can apply in order to escape if they are physically assaulted.

These prearranged techniques are analogous to grammar in language. By learning and repeatedly practicing basic rules, one will eventually be able to apply the techniques to different situations, spontaneously responding to the need to protect oneself. Grammar without application is not effective because it is no more than what it is—mere rules. However, by seriously practicing the prearranged forms of self-defense techniques one can learn numerous practical applications for them.

Repeated practice of the techniques with concentration and self-discipline will help children develop the mental strength that will shine in the form of self-confidence, self-awareness, self-reliance, responsible conduct, self-control, concentration, willpower, patience, self-discipline, and other valuable qualities. In this sense, self-defense practice is much more than just learning to defend oneself against an immediate attacker. Therefore, it is important to view self-defense instruction to children as a vehicle to teach them physical fitness, character development, safety education, self-defense techniques, and total self-development.

Here is an effective way to enhance a sense of self-worth. Sit on the floor with eyes closed. Breathe through the nose quietly and follow consciously each time when you breathe out.

CROSS SINGLE GRAB

1. Your partner's right hand grabs your right hand.

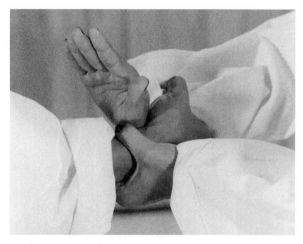

2. Grab your partner's right hand to stabilize it, and twist your right hand against the partner's right thumb in such a way that your right palm is placed on the top of the partner's right hand. Pull your right hand up and out of the grip.

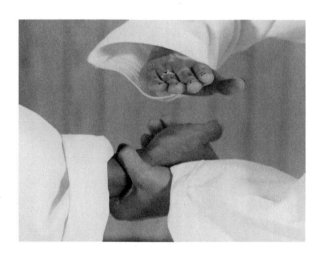

3. This technique should be practiced without any force. Step forward with the left foot if your left hand is held.

CROSS SINGLE GRAB

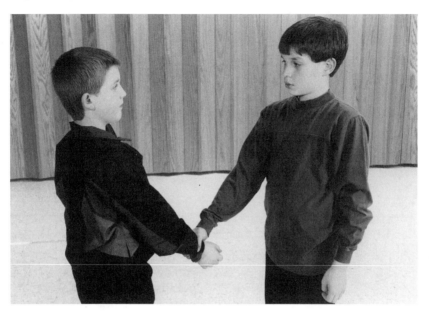

1. Your partner grabs your right hand with his right hand.

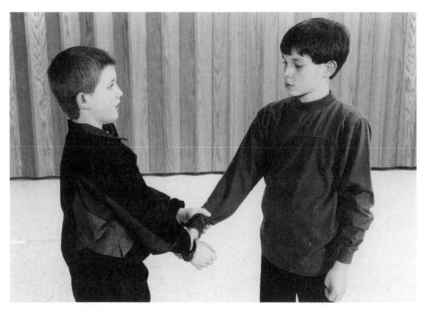

2. In order to free yourself from the partner's hold, grab the partner's right hand with your left hand to stabilize it.

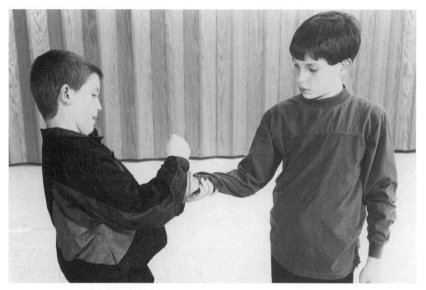

3. Twist your right hand against the right thumb of the partner. As soon as you take your right hand from the partner's grabbing hand, get away, run away, right away.

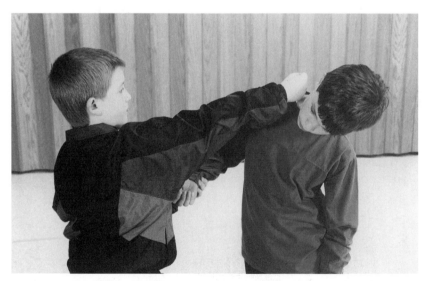

4. When a counterattack is absolutely necessary, a sideward backfist strike to the opponent's temple will be effective. When you practice the counterattack with the sideward backfist strike, make sure that *you do not touch your partner at all.*

STRAIGHT SINGLE GRAB

1. Your partner's right hand grabs your left hand.

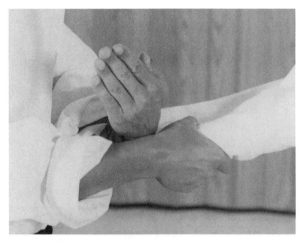

2. Grab your partner's right hand with your right hand to stabilize it. Twist your left hand against the partner's right thumb in such a way that your left palm faces upward, and pull your hand up and out of the grip.

3. As you execute this technique, your left elbow should stay close to your body. Step forward with your right foot if your partner grabs your right hand.

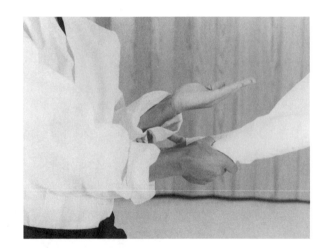

Just for Teachers and Parents

- Explain to children that because an infinite variety of self-defense situations is possible, the most effective way to learn self-defense techniques is to follow the basic patterns based on different self-defense situations. By understanding and practicing the fundamental prescribed techniques with diligence, children can learn how to deal with unexpected predicaments by their applications.
- Teach children that a good technique is based on scientific principles and not on brute force. Correct techniques are effective, and they transcend the sizes of people who use them.
- There is nothing like good hands-on instruction by an authentic teacher of the art of self-defense. If it is possible to receive such instruction, encourage children to do so. Although it is true that you can help children learn self-defense techniques through this book, it is not as beneficial alone as in conjunction with direct instruction by a good teacher.
- Teach children that mental discipline is more important than mere knowledge of physical techniques. During the practice of self-defense techniques, children must be taught to be serious and well-disciplined. Children will develop self-confidence and concentration if they follow the method described in this book. Patience and repetition are the keys for an effective practice.
- Because of the nature of the subject material, it goes without saying that safety is of the utmost importance in the practice of any self-defense technique. Teach children to practice the techniques in slow motion in the beginning. You can let them add speed and power gradually as they become familiar with each technique. Have them practice with self-control and an absolute respect for their partners.
- Teach children that during the practice of self-defense techniques, their mental state should be as if the situation were real. It is a part of the mental discipline through which children eventually become able to apply whatever they learn to various situations if forced to protect themselves. This may sound contradictory to the matter of safety in practice with slow motion stated above, but in reality there is no contradiction here. Self-discipline, concentration, self-respect, and respect for others are all important parts of learning self-defense.
- The techniques shown on the pages that follow are meant to be practiced with a partner and are most effective when performed exactly as described.

BASIC WRIST THROW

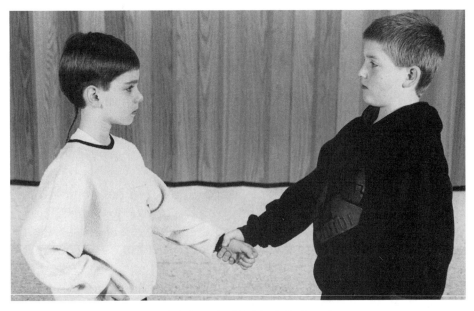

1. Your partner grabs your left hand with his right hand.

2. You grab your partner's right hand with your right hand, with your right thumb placed on the back of your partner's right hand.

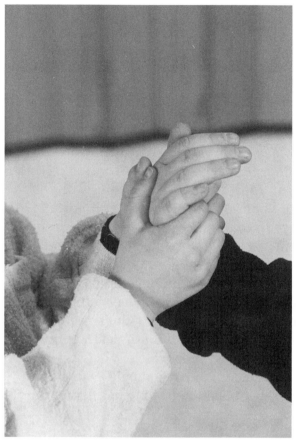

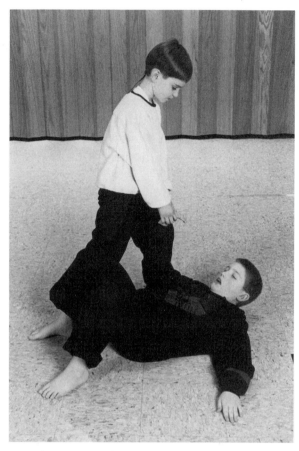

3. Free your left hand by twisting it against the partner's right thumb. Lift the partner's right hand as you place both thumbs behind your partner's right hand. Push your partner's right hand backward and apply pressure to his right wrist with both your hands.

4. When you take your partner down to the ground, make sure that the partner knows how to fall safely. Practice this technique and all other techniques slowly in the beginning for safety and better understanding.

Kids' Corner

In the practice of self-defense techniques on your own or with your friends, the most important thing is safety—your own safety and the safety of others involved in practicing. Now, it is true that in order to learn effective techniques, you are encouraged to execute techniques with real feeling and power in training. But for the sake of safety and better understanding of each technique, it is wise to practice each technique in slow motion in the beginning. Gradually, you can eventually execute the techniques with full power in cooperation with your partner.

Self-control is needed to practice techniques in safety. You must control your physical techniques as well as your mental attitude of mutual respect. It is necessary to create a good training program with your partners. Here is an important guideline: practice the technique as if it is real, and perform the technique in a real situation as if it is practice. What this means is that you must be serious and intense in practice, imagining that you are actually defending yourself against someone who tries to be violent to you. Then, in a real situation, your techniques become automatic and you can execute them in a calm and confident manner.

So enjoy the practice of self-defense techniques with your friends. But remember that safety is the number-one consideration in the practice of self-defense, and effectiveness of the techniques comes after that. The list of possible self-defense situations is endless, so you must practice the basic techniques repeatedly. One thing that we must remember is the importance of mental strength in actual usage of the self-defense techniques.

Your mental strength is, perhaps, more important than mere knowledge of the physical skills of self-defense. If you have no mental strength that keeps you calm, confident, and resourceful in a dangerous situation, your physical skill will be of no use. This is why direct instruction by a good teacher is important. He or she can teach you how to develop good techniques as well as how to develop your mind to be prepared for any situation.

Kiai

Shouting, screaming, and yelling can be an effective weapon in a dangerous situation. Sometimes it is possible to offset a perpetrator's aggression without any technique by mere shouting, if it is loud and strong.

In karate the traditional yell when attacking is called *kiai*. Kiai helps one to produce extra power and focus at the moment of execution of the technique. It enhances self-confidence and brings out additional energy from within.

For young children kiai can be simply a healthy, strong, confident shout. Encourage them to bring out a sound from the bottom of the stomach as they breathe out. The sound they should use in the beginning is similar to that of the number eight. Theoretically, one may use kiai in executing any technique, although in traditional martial arts training kiai is utilized in a certain manner. Encourage children to yell loudly to escape from an attack or unwanted advance from would-be offenders.

For older children kiai can be explained as a method of coordinating mental and physical powers through the exhalation of air through the lower abdomen. Actually, this method is used by many athletes in many different sports, although they may not be conscious of it, in order to maximize performance effectiveness.

It is healthy and effective to yell aloud as you execute each technique. Normally, for the execution of counterattacks such as punching or kicking for self-defense, you make a strong sound as you exhale air by placing power in your lower abdomen. You should place the same power in your lower abdomen as well as strong breathing out at the moment of blocking but you don't have to utter an audible sound when blocking.

Yell and shout as loudly as you can and let it come from your tan-den (lower abdomen) as you exhale air. It has a cleansing effect for fear and self-doubt. You will feel good and powerful when you execute a strong kiai because it can also serve as a means to release tension.

For those who wish to think of kiai at a philosophical level, it is an expression of self and, ultimately, asserting the self. It is saying who you are—claiming self-respect and asserting your value in this universe. It is a symbolic action in that breathing is the most important physiological function and that becomes the basis of kiai, which, in turn, becomes the method of asserting the existence of self on the earth.

DOUBLE-HAND STANDING GRAB

1. Your partner grabs both of your hands, which are raised upward.

2. In order to escape from his grab, first take one step forward to assure your balance; then twist your hands downward against your partner's thumbs.

3. Pull your hands sideward as if you are showing the "safe" gesture used by umpires in baseball. Don't forget—"get away, run away, right away" in a real situation.

DOUBLE-HAND STRAIGHT GRAB

1. Your partner grabs your hands with both of his hands.

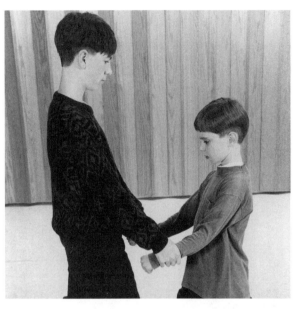

2. In order to free your hands from this grab, first take one step forward to assure your balance.

3. Twist your hands against both the partner's thumbs in such a way that your fists show their palm sides upward.

4. Pull your hands sideward first and then toward you. Get away, run away, right away.

ONE-ARM GRAB

1. Your partner grabs your right arm with both of his hands.

2. In order to free your right hand from your partner's hands, take one step forward with your right foot and grab your own right hand with your left hand from above.

3. Pull both of your hands to the middle of your chest as you move your left foot to line it up with your right foot.

4. After you free your right hand with this method, you may run away or, if it is absolutely necessary, you may counterattack with a back-fist strike or front kick to the lower stomach of your opponent. Always be sure to avoid contact in practice.

ONE-ARM GRAB

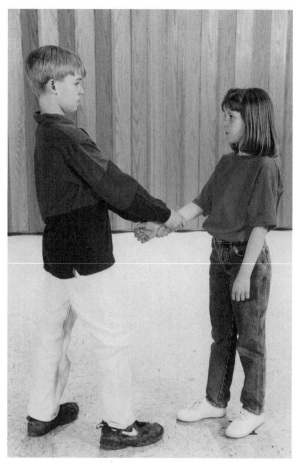 

1. Your partner grabs your right arm with both of his hands.

2. Take one step forward with your right foot as you clasp your hands by bringing your left hand between the partner's hands from above.

3. By moving your left foot, place your feet in a straight line. At the same time, pull your hands to your chest. Get away, run away, right away. Practice this technique and all other techniques for both sides, right and left.

CHOKE OR GRAB FROM FRONT

1. Your partner places two hands on your neck, simulating choking or grabbing.

2. First, clasp your hands as if you were shaking hands with yourself.

3. Then squat down, keeping your back straight.

4. Raise your clasped hands straight up to take your partner's hands off your neck. Your elbows should be open slightly wider than your head—as if you were diving—as you wedge your partner's hands off. (One can then run away, or counterattack if absolutely necessary.)

CHOKE OR GRAB FROM FRONT WITH COUNTERATTACK

1. Your partner places both hands on your shoulders with some force, simulating choking situation.

2. Squat down with hands clasped and your back straight.

3. Spring up with the strength of your knees, hips, and lower abdomen. Break your partner's choke hold by pushing up your arms like a wedge.

4. Execute the front elbow strike to your partner's midsection (solar plexus) in a square squat-down stance as shown.

5. Place your right knee down on the ground as you place your right forearm to the inner side of your partner's knee.

6. Pull your partner's right foot with your left hand while you push the inner side of your partner's right knee with your right forearm.

7. The motions of pushing the right knee and pulling the right foot should be synchronized in order to execute an effective throw. Perform this technique and all other techniques slowly in the beginning for safety in practice, gradually increasing power and speed as you attain more control.

CHOKE OR GRAB FROM FRONT WITH COUNTERATTACK

1. Your partner places his hands on your shoulders or neck, simulating a choking or grabbing motion.

2. In order to escape from his grab or choke, first squat down with your back as straight as possible and clasp your hands tightly.

3. As you come upward to break your partner's hold by the wedge of your arms, utilize the synchronized power of your hips, knees, and lower abdomen.

4. Get away, run away, right away. But if you are forced to execute a counterattack technique after you free yourself from his grabbing or choking motion, a front elbow strike to your partner's solar plexus will be effective. Make sure that you practice this technique and all other techniques with an absolute no-contact rule.

CHOKE OR GRAB FROM BEHIND

1. Your partner places both hands on your shoulders from behind, simulating a choking or grabbing motion.

2. To free yourself from your partner's hold, first bring your right foot back slightly closer to your left heel.

3. Move your left foot forward in such a way that it lines up with your right foot and your partner. At the same time, bring both of your hands to shoulder level with palms facing toward you. Your hands can be open, as shown here, or in fists, as on page 140.

4. Spin your body clockwise as you turn your hands to show their palms to the partner. You must shift your weight to the left leg as you break the partner's hands off your back. Keep your feet firmly placed as you turn. Practice this technique and all other techniques in a slow motion first for safety and better understanding of the technique. Practice both right and left sides.

CHOKE OR GRAB FROM BEHIND

1. Your partner places both of his hands on your shoulders or neck from behind, simulating a grabbing or choking motion.

2. In order to free yourself from his hold, first bring your right foot back slightly closer to your left heel.

3. Next, move your left foot forward to place it in line with your right foot. Bend your arms with the fists showing their palm sides toward you.

4. As you spin clockwise, shift your weight to your left foot and parry off your partner's right hand from your back. Practice this technique and all other techniques for both sides, right and left. In a real situation you must get away, run away, right away.

CHOKE OR GRAB FROM BEHIND

1. Your partner places both of his hands on your shoulders from behind, simulating a choking or grabbing motion.

2. To escape from the attack, bring your right foot slightly back to the inside of your partner's front foot. Next bring your left foot forward in line with your right foot. Both your arms are high, prepared to spin and break off the partner's hold.

3. As you spin your upper body clockwise, keep your weight on your left leg and take off your partner's grabbing arms with your right forearm. Your fists show their palm sides toward you in the preparatory position, and at the moment of contact with your partner's arms, the palms face your partner.

4. Grab your partner's right hand with your right hand to execute a follow-up technique.

5. An effective counterattack in this case will be a right roundhouse knee attack to your partner's solar plexus (no contact in practice).

Kids' Corner

It is OK to get angry sometimes. It is natural that we all have some bad times once in a while—something we don't agree with, somebody we don't like, or some unkind thing said about us, especially if it is untrue.

But the important thing is to express our anger in a constructive manner. We should not act in a way that we may regret later, and we should not want to do something that will hurt others. Human beings are different from other animals like dogs and cats—we don't react to things and people with impulse. We must think before we act.

If you have a disagreement with your friends, talk about it. Even yelling at each other is better than using physical violence. If it is difficult to talk by yourselves, ask other friends or teachers to mediate, and try to communicate with adversaries through them. It is one of our human privileges that we can rationally exchange words to solve problems. So use words, not violence, to work out your problems. It is not always easy to talk with someone you don't like at the moment. Words can make you feel bad, too. But, at least you are acting like a civilized human being, and that is important.

When you become angry, it is good to keep yourself busy with an activity that you enjoy. This is a wonderful way to release and forget your anger. Another effective way to deal with anger is to write down your angry feelings. Put down on paper why and how you are angry as well as what and who made you angry, and so on. And of course, if you have a chance, you should talk about your feelings to someone who listens to you. This will help you sort out the situation, and you will feel less angry about it, too. Try to express your angry feelings in a constructive way and not in a destructive way.

So let's not act on impulse. Before you act with anger, take three deep breaths and think about it. Remember that a truly strong person is one who can control himself or herself.

ESCAPING AN ATTACK FROM BEHIND, FOLLOWED BY OUTER MAJOR SWEEP

1. Your partner places both hands on your shoulders or neck, simulating an attack by choking or grabbing from behind.

2. Move your right foot slightly back, closer to your partner, and bring your left foot forward in such a way that your two feet are placed in a line with your partner.

3. Turn clockwise to deflect or parry off your partner's hold with your right arm. Your weight is shifted to your left leg at the moment you parry off your partner's hold.

4. Bring your left foot outside of your partner's right foot, simultaneously placing your right hand to your partner's left jaw. Your left hand keeps holding your partner's right arm.

5. Bring your right leg behind your partner's right leg to get ready to sweep it.

6. In sweeping your partner's right leg with your right leg, make sure that your right calf makes contact with your partner's right calf. Practice this technique and all other techniques in slow motion in the beginning.

ATTACK FROM BEHIND TO INNER SWEEP

1. As your partner places both hands on your back, simulating a choking or grabbing attack from behind, move your right foot slightly back toward your partner and bring your left foot forward in such a way that your two feet are placed in a straight line.

2. Turn clockwise with both arms in ready-to-defend position, parrying off your partner's hold with your right arm. Your weight is distributed more on your left leg at this moment.

3. Grab your partner's right arm with your right hand. Bring your left foot outside your partner's left foot and execute the right roundhouse knee kick to your partner's midsection. Practice this technique and all other techniques with full control and with no contact for the sake of safety. Practice all techniques on both the right and left sides.

4. For a follow-up technique, place your right foot outside your partner's right foot as you keep holding your partner's right arm with your right hand. Your left hand is placed behind your partner's neck at this moment.

5. The back of your left knee makes contact with the inside of your partner's right knee. Synchronize the sweeping motion, pushing your partner's head downward and pulling his right arm with your right hand for an effective throw.

6. As you finish the throwing technique, let your partner fall gently. Practice this technique and all other techniques in slow motion in the beginning. If you are taking a fall, remember to turn your face to the side as you fall to protect your face from striking the floor. (This photo does not show proper falling technique [ukemi] explained earlier. The important thing is to practice in slow motion for safety's sake.)

UPPER BLOCK TO OUTER MAJOR SWEEP

1. Block your partner's upper lunge punch from the natural stance.

2. Grab your partner's attacking hand with your blocking hand. Place your right open hand on your partner's left jaw, and at the same time bring your left foot next to your partner's right foot.

4. Synchronize the motions of sweeping your partner's right leg, pulling your partner's right arm, and pushing his left jaw.

3. Break your partner's balance by pulling down his right arm and pushing his left jaw as you prepare to sweep his right leg with your right leg.

5. Keep holding your partner's right arm as you complete the technique. Perform this technique and all others in slow motion in the beginning. Make sure that your partner is familiar with falling techniques before you throw him.

UPPER BLOCK TO OUTER MAJOR SWEEP (METHOD A)

1. Block your partner's upper attack with your left arm. (In a real situation, this can be a grabbing attempt by a bully.)

2. Grab the attacking arm with your blocking hand and execute an upper elbow strike to your partner's chin (no contact in practice).

4. In throwing, your right calf makes contact with your partner's right calf. As you sweep your partner's leg, try to have the sensation of drawing an arc on the floor with your right toes.

3. Move your left foot next to your partner's right foot as you place your right hand on your partner's left jaw. In this photo, the defender is already prepared to sweep her partner's right leg with her right leg.

UPPER BLOCK TO OUTER MAJOR SWEEP (METHOD B)

1. You and your partner face each other with hands high as shown.

2. Block your partner's right upper punch with your left arm.

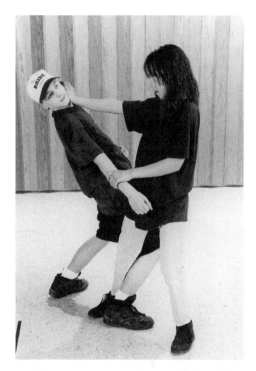

3. Grab the attacking arm with your blocking arm and bring your left foot forward outside of your partner's right foot. At the same time, place your open hand on your partner's left jaw.

4. Throw your partner on his back by sweeping his right leg with your right leg and by pushing your right hand against his left jaw as you pull down his right arm.

5. Make sure that your partner knows how to fall correctly before you throw him. Practice this technique and all other techniques in slow motion in the beginning for safety as well as for better understanding.

UPPER BLOCK TO OUTER MAJOR SWEEP (METHOD C)

1. Block your partner's right upper punch with your right arm.

2. Grab your partner's attacking arm and bring it down with both of your hands.

3. Move your left foot outside of and next to your partner's right foot as you place your right open hand on your partner's left jaw.

4. Bring your right leg behind your partner's right leg and keep breaking his balance as you prepare to sweep his leg.

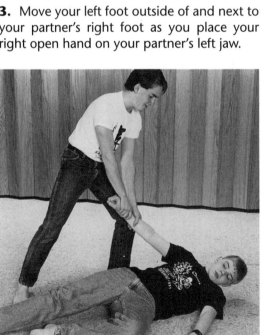

5. As you complete the throw, keep holding your partner's right arm. Make sure that your partner knows how to fall before you throw him. Practice this technique and all others in slow motion in the beginning.

TWO-HAND GRAB FROM BEHIND

1. Your partner grabs your hands from behind as shown here.

2. Lift your left arm high and twist your upper body to come under your partner's left arm.

3. As you finish twisting, your partner's left hand leaves your left hand. You immediately place your freed left hand on the top of your partner's right hand to grab it.

4. Twist your partner's right hand upward with both of your hands. Both of your thumbs meet at the back of your partner's right hand.

5. Step forward with your left foot as you continue to apply pressure to your partner's wrist, twisting it backward.

6. In practice, put your partner down gently, especially in the beginning, for safety and better understanding of the technique.

7. If you keep holding the partner's right hand and bend the wrist, this technique becomes a submission (holding) method as well. Practice it for both sides, right and left.

TWO-HAND GRAB FROM BEHIND (METHOD A)

1. Your partner grabs both of your hands from behind.

2. To free your hands, take one step with your left foot to the left side with a swinging motion of your left arm above your head as shown.

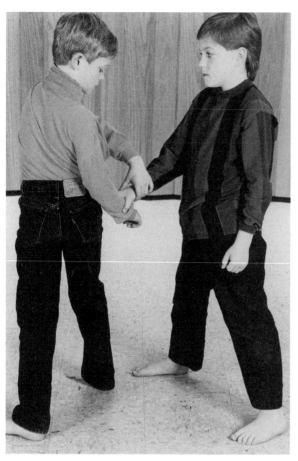

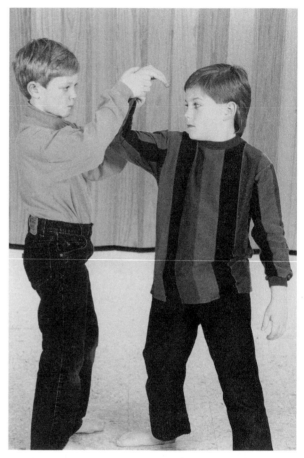

3. As you turn your right side, place your left thumb on the back of your partner's right hand.

4. Free your right hand as you push it against your partner's right thumb. Place your right thumb on the back of your partner's right hand next to your left thumb.

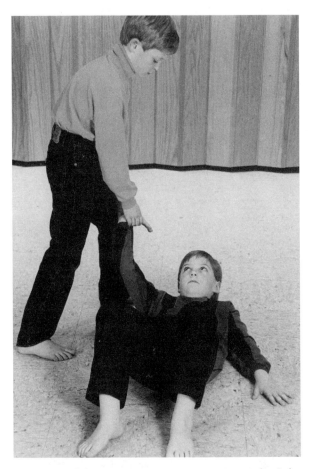

5. By applying pressure on your partner's right wrist with both of your hands, throw him on his back. Practice this technique and all other techniques in slow motion in the beginning for safety and better understanding.

TWO-HAND GRAB FROM BEHIND (METHOD B)

1. Your partner grabs both of your hands from behind as shown.

2. In order to free your hands, first raise your left hand high as you step your left foot to the left side.

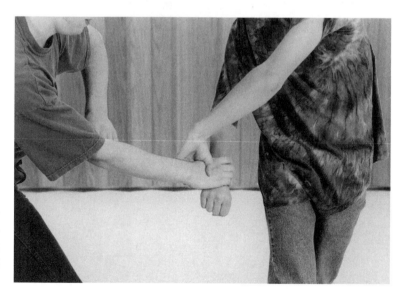

3. Turn to the right and place your left thumb on the back of your partner's right hand. Twist your right hand against your partner's right thumb to free it.

4. Place your right thumb on the back of your partner's right hand next to your left thumb. Bend your partner's right hand by pressuring its wrist.

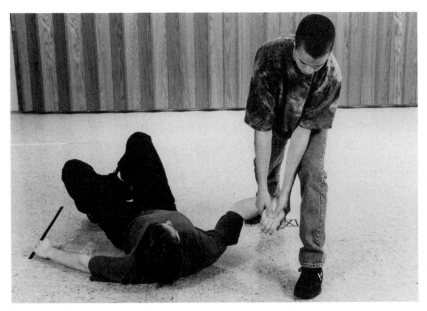

5. As you step forward with your left foot, throw your partner on his back by continuous pressure on his right wrist with both hands. Practice this technique gently in the beginning for safety as well as for better understanding.

Kids' Corner

When you know and believe that you are good, important, and worth being respected, your conduct becomes the same—good, important, and worth being respected. This feeling of self-importance is not arrogance, selfishness, or self-centeredness. This comes from a genuine feeling that you are a member of the human community and that we all have a part to play in improving the society in which we live. Society consists of individuals, and a good society consists of good individuals.

Respect for oneself makes it possible to respect others. It is particularly important to remember that we must respect our parents and teachers. By showing respect for parents and teachers, we are showing respect for ourselves as well, for they care about us and guide us in the right direction. They deserve our respect. So respect goes around and comes around, starting with self-respect.

A person with self-respect cares about herself enough not to do anything to deliberately hurt herself. Therefore, it goes without saying that thinking of taking drugs or "experimenting" with drugs is out of the question for someone with self-respect. Hundreds of thousands of people have shown that drugs hurt them—they have demonstrated with their own lives how dangerous illegal drugs are. If we don't learn from their mistakes, we lack self-respect and intelligence. No one has to "experiment" with drugs—it has been done already by so many people, with terrible results.

When the concept of mutual respect is practiced, it goes without saying that violent behavior among young people disappears or at least occurs less frequently. If we respect each other, how can we hurt each other by using violence? Treat each other like respectable and respected human beings instead of animals, and we will automatically refrain from using violence toward each other.

UPPER ELBOW STRIKE

1. You and your partner face each other with a ready-to-practice posture, simulating basic defensive and offensive postures.

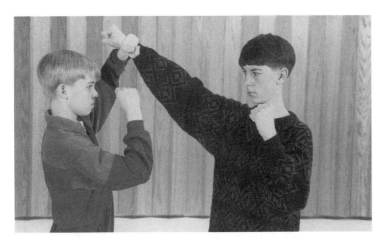

2. Block your partner's right upper punch with your left arm.

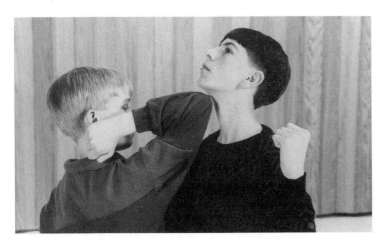

3. Grab the attacking arm and execute the right upper elbow strike to your partner's chin or solar plexus. Your right fist shows its palm side toward your right ear. Make sure that an absolute no-contact rule is practiced. Learn this technique and all other techniques on both sides, right and left. Practice in slow motion for safety and effective learning.

DEFENDING AN ATTACK FROM YOUR RIGHT SIDE

1. Your partner stands with a ready-to-attack posture on your right side.

2. Block your partner's right upper punch with your right arm.

3. Grab the attacking arm with your left hand.

4. Slide toward your partner as you keep holding his right hand with your left hand, and prepare to execute the side elbow strike.

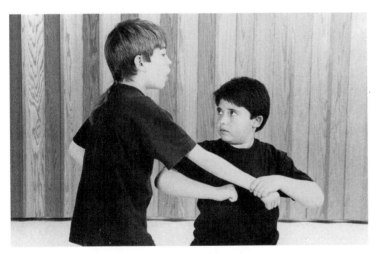

5. Execute a side elbow strike to your partner's midsection. (No contact in practice.) Practice this technique and all other techniques in slow motion in the beginning for safety and better understanding.

Kids' Corner

Self-confidence is important if you want to accomplish something or excel in any field. Self-confidence does not come from nowhere—it comes from believing in yourself. And, naturally, you've got to try your best at whatever you are doing—schoolwork, sports, music, art, or anything else. When you truly know that you can do something and that you know something, your self-confidence shines. Sometimes it is good enough to know that you have done your best in accomplishing something, regardless of its results, to add to your confidence.

Self-confidence can help you in all sorts of ways. For example, when someone accuses you of something you have not done, or when you are confronted by bullies threatening to take money from you, you can take care of yourself if you have true self-confidence. First of all, when you know that you are right, you will not be afraid of anything or anybody. You believe in yourself 100 percent because you are right. Your self-confidence will permeate through your total self and it will show to others that you don't deserve accusation or blame for something you have not done.

When confronted by bullies, you may try a couple of different tactics to protect yourself. First of all, try to negotiate with them. Talk to them not with fear, but with self-confidence. Your self-confidence in this case comes from your belief that you have not done anything wrong to anyone and you don't deserve to be harassed by those bullies. You may tell them that you don't have any money to give to them, and perhaps you may ask them if they want to work somewhere if they need money. You may volunteer to talk to a teacher or counselor on their behalf on this matter. When they realize that you are not afraid of them but you show them proper respect as friends, you may be surprised to find that they back off and leave you alone.

If you want to carry self-confidence all the time in your attitude and behavior, you must act with self-respect and respect for others. This requires some self-discipline because there are many occasions when your attitude of self-respect and respect for others will be tested.

DEFENDING AN ATTACK FROM YOUR LEFT SIDE (METHOD A)

1. Your partner is ready to attack you from your left side.

2. Block your partner's right punch with your left arm.

3. Grab the attacking arm immediately with your right hand.

4. Slide toward your partner as you keep holding his right hand. Execute the left side elbow strike to his rib area.

5. Bring your left arm across your partner's upper chest. Try to feel as if you are placing your left hand on his left shoulder area.

6. Press your partner's right leg with your left knee and simultaneously push him backward with your left arm. Make sure that your partner knows how to fall properly. Practice this technique and all others in slow motion in the beginning for safety and better understanding.

DEFENDING AN ATTACK FROM YOUR LEFT SIDE (METHOD B)

1. Your partner attacks you from your left side with his left upper punch. You block with your left arm.

2. As soon as you block his left punch, grab his arm with your right hand.

3. Slide toward your partner and execute the left side elbow strike to his rib area. Squat down as you see here for balance and stability as you execute the side elbow strike.

4. Get down on your left knee and place your left forearm on the inside of your partner's left knee and grab his left foot at its ankle with your right hand.

5. Pull your right hand toward you as you push your left forearm against the inner side of your partner's knee.

SUBMISSION HOLD

1. Block your partner's right upper punch with your left arm.

2. Grab your partner's attacking arm with your right hand while your left hand is prepared to execute a backfist strike.

3. Execute a backfist strike to your partner's face (no contact in practice).

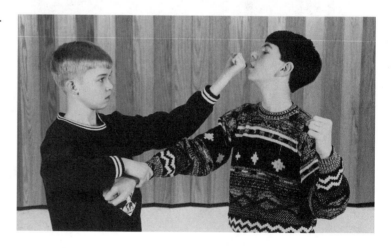

4. Bring your left foot close to your partner's right foot as you place your left forearm on the back of your partner's right elbow.

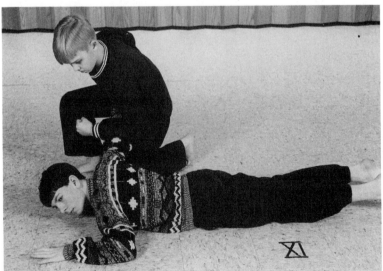

5. Submission is complete when you place your left knee on the ground as you place pressure on your partner's right elbow with your left forearm. Keep your partner's right hand on your right thigh.

STANDING SUBMISSION

1. You and your partner face each other in the ready-to-practice position.

2. Your partner steps in with his right foot and executes a right upper punch. You block the attack with your right arm.

3. Grab the attacking arm immediately with your left hand and execute a backfist thrust attack to your partner's face. (Absolutely no contact in practice.)

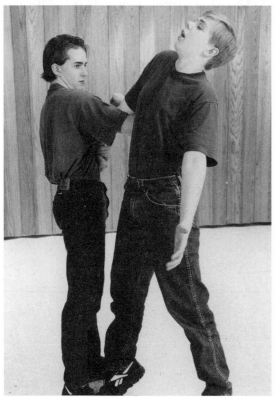

4. Bring your right forearm under your partner's right elbow and push it up. Keep holding your partner's right hand downward with your left hand.

Kids' Corner

Unfortunately, there are a lot of violent scenes on TV and in movies. What you must remember is that most of those scenes are not real; and even if it is claimed that some of the scenes represent a true occurrence, they should not have happened anyway. In our society violence in any form should not be tolerated. Violence creates pain and suffering for everyone involved and it never solves problems. We human beings should be ashamed that any violence exists in our world.

In order to create a world free of violence, interpersonal as well as global, we must start with a grass-roots effort, creating a peaceful atmosphere in environments close to us such as schools, homes, and neighborhoods. We must learn how to solve conflicts without violence but with talk and negotiation. By maintaining self-respect and mutual respect, we can behave as civilized people without fear of violence.

You should not act with violence toward anyone, and at the same time you should not become a victim of violence by others. Once we understand that violence is stupid and degrading, chances are that even violent kids will become less violent or not violent at all. It is our hope that someday all human beings on earth will learn the absurdity of violence and that there will be no need for us to fear violence anywhere.

But self-defense is important, and you must be aware that you have to protect yourself if you are placed in danger. There is a big difference between violence and self-defense. In self-defense, you are forced to use techniques—mental and physical—to save yourself from harmful acts of violent individuals. If the time comes when you know that you cannot run away or walk away and have to defend yourself, you have to act with confidence and concentration to protect yourself. This book gives you the basic necessary techniques as well as information that will enable you to protect yourself if the need arises. You must practice the techniques diligently. If you have a chance to attend a self-defense class taught by a professional instructor, you should take advantage of such an opportunity. There is no substitute for good hands-on instruction by experienced instructors.

GROUND SUBMISSION

1. Block your partner's right upper punch with your right arm from the natural stance.

2. Grab your partner's attacking arm with your blocking arm. Pull down your partner's right arm as you place your left foot next to his right foot, simultaneously pushing the back of your partner's right elbow with your left forearm.

3. As you shift your weight to your right leg, keep constant pressure on the back of your partner's right elbow with your left forearm.

4. At the completion of the technique, your left knee (closer to your partner) is on the ground and your right foot is at your partner's face level. Place your partner's right arm tightly on your right thigh as you continue to apply pressure on the back of his right elbow.

5. Apply pressure on the correct spot, just behind the back of his elbow. Practice this technique and all other techniques on both sides (attack from the right and from the left).

BASIC WRIST THROW

1. Your partner grabs your right hand with his right hand. (Practice this technique and all other techniques on both sides, right and left.)

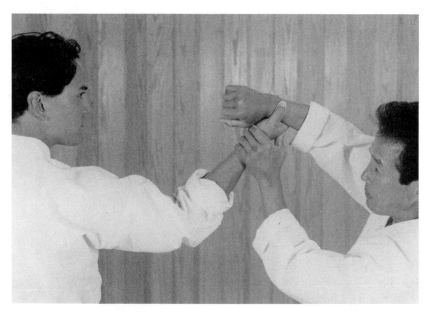

2. Lift up your right hand as your partner keeps holding on to it. Place your left hand behind your partner's right hand.

3. Press your partner's right hand back with your left thumb, as you take your right hand out of your partner's hold.

4. Now place both thumbs behind your partner's right hand and press it backward by applying pressure on the wrist with both hands.

5. Throw your partner backward gently by applying extra pressure on his wrist. Make sure that your partner knows how to fall before you throw him. Step in with your left foot in this case. When you execute this technique on the other side, you step in with your right foot.

6. Perform this technique and all others in slow motion in the beginning for safety and better understanding.

SPINNING WRIST THROW

1. Your partner grabs your left hand with his right hand.

2. Move your left hand counterclockwise and grab the back of your partner's right hand.

3. Grab your partner's right hand with both of your hands.

4. With your left foot as the center of pivoting counterclockwise, bring your right foot closer to your partner's right foot by turning your body underneath your partner's right arm.

5. As you finish turning, you are holding your partner's wrist in a ready-to-throw position.

6. Apply pressure to your partner's wrist as well as to the arm by means of your right elbow. Bring your left foot forward as you execute the throw.

7. Practice this technique and all others in slow, gentle motion in the beginning for safety as well as better understanding.

A CLOSER LOOK AT THE SPINNING WRIST THROW

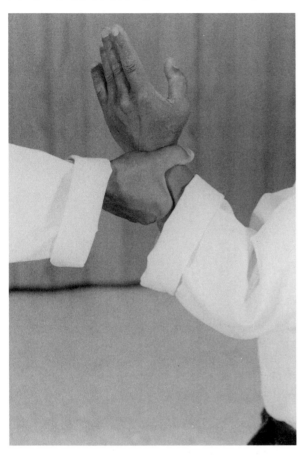 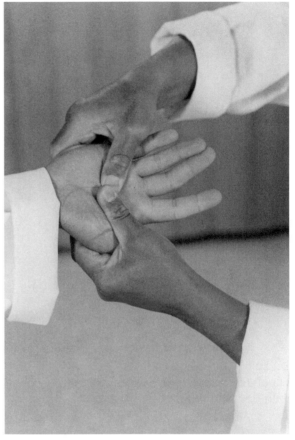

1. Your partner grabs your left hand with his right hand.

2. Rotate your left hand counterclockwise (against your partner's right thumb) and grab the back of his right hand in such a way as to place your left thumb at the middle of his right palm. Your right thumb is now placed next to your left thumb.

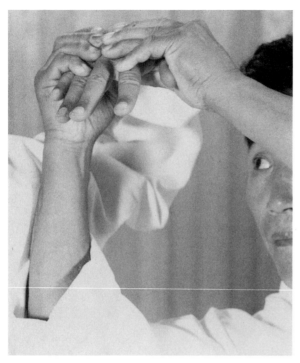

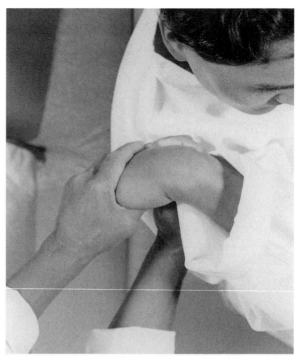

3. Spin your whole body under his right arm counterclockwise as you keep holding his hand with both thumbs on his right palm.

4. Press your partner's right wrist backward with both of your hands.

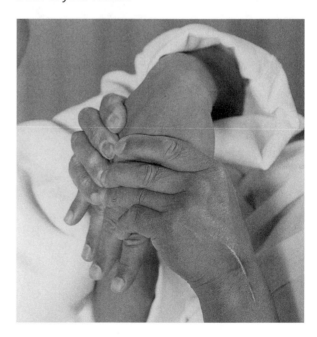

5. Pressure is applied on your partner's right wrist as well as his shoulder and arm by pressing your right arm against his right arm from underneath.

ONE-ARM CHOKE TO SHOULDER THROW

1. Pull your chin down as your partner attempts to choke you from behind with his right arm.

2. Grab your partner's right arm with your right hand, and bring your right foot inside his right foot.

3. Move your left foot back closer to your partner's left foot. At this moment, you may execute the back elbow strike to the partner's midsection. Make sure that both of your knees are sufficiently bent.

4. In order to execute an effective throw, you must synchronize three factors: the springing motion of the knees, the strength of the hips, and the pulling of your right arm.

5. Make sure that your partner knows how to fall before you throw him.

6. Your right hand keeps holding your partner's right arm throughout the throw. Practice this technique and all other techniques in slow motion in the beginning. Practice falling technique before the actual throw.

HIP THROW

1. You evade your partner's upper punch by bending your upper body forward. Your right hand at this point is ready to block your partner's second punch.

2. Bring your left foot to the inside of your partner's left foot, and at the same time move your right foot to the inside of your partner's right foot. Hold your partner's left arm with your right hand and bring your left arm around your partner's lower back.

3. By synchronizing the actions of your knees, hips, and arms, throw your partner over your lower back.

4. Make sure that your partner knows how to fall before you throw him. Practice this technique in slow motion in the beginning.

5. Keep holding onto your partner's left arm as you finish the throw. Execution of the technique in slow motion is just as effective in learning, and moreover, it's a safe way to practice.

UPPER BLOCK TO SCISSORS THROW

1. Block your partner's right upper lunge attack with your left arm by stepping back with your right foot and assuming a half-and-half stance.

2. Grab your partner's right arm with your left hand and bring your right foot slightly closer to your partner's right foot. Execute a hook kick to your partner's midsection with your left foot (heel). In order to execute a proper hook kick, first bring your kicking leg up to your hip level with its knee bent. Your kicking foot should be about two shoulder lengths away from your partner's chest area. Throw the foot to your partner's solar plexus (midsection) with a snapping motion of the knee. Make sure that you do not make any contact in practice.

3. After execution of the hook kick, get down on both hands to prepare for a scissors throw.

4. Place your left leg in front of your partner's lower abdomen and your right leg behind your partner's right leg as shown.

5. As you maintain the scissors position against your partner's right leg, rotate your whole body counterclockwise until your partner falls on his back.

6. The scissors throw can be applied in such a way that your partner falls on his front as well. Make sure that your partner knows how to fall before you execute this technique on him. Practice this technique and all others in slow motion for the sake of absolute safety and better understanding of the techniques.

ONE-ARM SHOULDER THROW

1. Block your partner's right upper lunge punch with your left arm. (Practice this technique and all other techniques on both sides, right and left.)

2. Execute the right reverse punch to "freeze" your partner. (In practice, make sure that you keep the no-contact rule for absolute safety in all techniques.)

3. Bring your right foot to the inside of your partner's right foot. Keep holding your partner's attacking arm (the right arm, in this case) with both hands as shown.

4. Move your left foot all the way back to the inside of your partner's left foot. Squat down as you hold your partner's right arm on your right shoulder.

5. As you come up with both knees, pull your partner's right arm over your right shoulder. Your right hip must be pushed to the right to lift up your partner's body easily.

6. Hold on to your partner's right arm as you complete this technique. Make sure that your partner knows how to fall before you try this technique on him. Try to execute the technique as slowly as possible for safety as well as better understanding.

INNER MAJOR SWEEP

1. Your partner simulates a choking situation by placing both hands on your shoulders. (His right foot is forward.)

2. Squat down with your hands tightly clasped.

3. Break off the choke hold with your wedged arms by springing up with force from your knees, hips, and lower abdomen.

  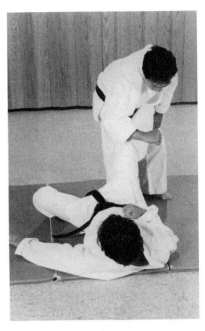

4. Hold your partner's right leg with your left hand as you come closer to him. Hook around your partner's left leg from inside with your right leg as shown. Your right forearm and elbow push your partner's midsection.

5. Sweep your partner's left leg with your right leg as you keep holding on to your partner's right leg with your left hand. Your right forearm and elbow push your partner's midsection simultaneously.

6. Make sure that your partner knows how to fall before you throw him. Execute this technique and all other techniques in slow motion for safety as well as better understanding.

DEFENDING AGAINST A ONE-ARM CHOKE (METHOD A)

1. Your partner chokes you from behind with his right arm. Pull your chin down immediately and grab the choking arm with your right hand.

2. Raise your left hand high as though you were trying to reach your partner's left shoulder. Move your right foot to outside of the partner's right foot.

3. Bring your left leg behind the partner's right leg. Push the partner's right knee from its back with your left knee.

4. Throw your partner by synchronizing your left knee's pushing motion, your left arm's pushing motion, and your hip's twisting motion.

5. Your right foot is stationary and works as the pivoting foot. Bring your left foot clockwise after you throw your partner. Hold your partner's right hand with both hands.

6. If a follow-up technique is absolutely needed, a kick to the partner's head or stomach can be executed. Make sure there is no contact in practice.

DEFENDING AGAINST A ONE-ARM CHOKE (METHOD B)

1. Your partner chokes you from behind with his right arm. Pull your chin down immediately and grab the choking arm with your right hand.

2. Bring your left foot closer to your right foot.

3. Move your right foot forward.

4. Twist your body and head clockwise. Push your head against your partner's midsection as you twist it.

5. As you escape from the hold, keep holding your partner's right arm and shoulder with both hands.

6. Execute the right front knee kick to your partner's midsection. (No contact in practice.)

DEFENDING AGAINST A BEAR HUG (FRONT VIEW)

1. Your partner holds you from behind with a bear hug.

2. Relax your body and arms. Clasp your hands and push them downward with both elbows tightly rubbing your lower ribs.

3. Bring your left foot next to your right foot. Move your right foot forward as you twist your upper body clockwise. Push your head against your partner's chest area.

4. Keep twisting your upper body until you are free of your partner's hold. Recover your balance immediately to get away from the "opponent" or counterattack him.

DEFENDING AGAINST A BEAR HUG (SIDE VIEW)

1. Your partner holds you from behind with a bear hug.

2. Relax your body and arms. Clasp your hands and push them downward with both elbows tightly rubbing your lower ribs.

3. Move your right foot closer to your partner's right foot.

4. Push your lower body forward.

5. Step forward with your right foot as you twist your body clockwise to escape from his hold.

DEFENDING AGAINST A HEADLOCK

1. Your partner holds your neck from your left side with his right arm.

2. Grab his right arm with your right hand as you push his lower ribs with your left hand. Bring your right foot forward.

3. Twist your head clockwise as you push it against your partner's right armpit, simultaneously pushing his right lower ribs with your left hand.

4. When you finish escaping from your partner's headlock, keep your left foot next to his right foot.

5. Bring your right arm up to hold the partner's neck.

6. Bring your right foot behind the partner's right foot, preparing for an outer major sweep.

7. As you throw your partner, keep holding him for a correct finish of the technique.

Index

Abdominal exercises, 34–36
Anger, 2–3, 143
Arm exercises, 22–23
Attacks
   defending, from left side, 171–75
   defending, from right side, 168–69
Attacks from behind
   escaping from, by inner sweep, 147–49
   escaping from, by outer major sweep,
     144–46
Attention stance, 41–43

Back elbow strike, 78
Back falling method, 108–10
Back kicks, 96–99
Backfist strike, 71
Balance, breathing and, 3
Bear hug, defending against, 208–11
Block techniques
   downward, 63–64
   inside-outward, 65–66
   outside-inward, 67–69
   upper, 60–62
   upper, to scissors throw, 196–98
Blocking
   kicks, 49
   punches, 50
Breathe in–breathe out exercise,
    10–11
Breathing, 3
Bullies, 5–6, 170

Cardiovascular exercises, 37–38
Character, developing sound, 3
Choke holds
   defending against one-arm, 204–7
   one-arm, to shoulder throw, 191–93
Conflict resolution, 2
Cross single grab, 115–17

Double-hand standing grab, 124
Double-hand straight grab, 125
Downward block, 63–64
Downward elbow strike, 79–81
Drugs, 166

Elbow strikes
   back, 78
   downward, 79–81
   front, 72–73
   side, 76–77
   upper, 74–75, 167
Escape techniques, 113

Falling methods, 103
   back, 108–10
   front, 106–7
   front rolling, 111–12
   side, 104–5
Fight or flight reaction, 1
Fist techniques, 52–55
Front elbow strike, 72–73
Front falling method, 106–7

Front kick, 82–87
Front rolling falling method, 111–12
Front stance, 42, 46
    and defending from natural stance,
      49
    with downward block, 48
    with lunge punch, 48

Grab techniques
    from behind, 138–42
    choke, 130–31
    choke, with counterattack, 132–37
    choke from behind, 138–42
    cross single, 115–17
    double-hand standing, 124
    double-hand straight, 125
    from front, 130–31
    from front with counterattack,
      132–37
    one-arm, 126–29
    straight single, 118–19
    two-hand, from behind, 158–65
Grounded submission hold, 181–82

Half-and-half stance, 42
    blocking kicks from, 49
    blocking punches from, 50
Headlocks, defending against,
    212–14
Hip throw, 194–95

Inner major sweep, 202–3
Inner peace, 3
Inside-outward block, 65–66

Kiai, 123
Kick techniques
    back, 96–99
    front, 82–85
    roundhouse, 92–95
    roundhouse knee, 100–1
    side, 86–91
Knee exercises, 39–40

Leg exercises, 30–33

Martial arts, self-defense and, 5
Mental discipline, 119
Mental self-defense, 4
Movies, violence in, 2, 180
Mutual bow, 44
Mutual respect, 166

Natural stance, 42, 45
    defending from, and front-stance attack,
      49
Neck exercise, 24–25
Non-violence, 1–2

One-arm choke holds
    defending against, 204–7
    to shoulder throw, 191–93
One-arm grab, 126–29
One-arm shoulder throw, 199–201
Outer major sweeps
    escaping attack with, 144–47
    from upper blocks, 150–57
Outside-inward block, 67–69
    backfist strike and, 71

Peace, inner, 3
Personal strength, 6–8
Posture, 3
Practice, 113–14
    safety and, 122
Punch and block combination techniques
    back elbow strike, 78
    downward elbow strike, 79–81
    front elbow strike, 72–73
    outside-inward block and backfist strike,
      71
    side elbow strike, 76–77
    upper block and basic punch,
      70
    upper elbow strike, 74–75
Punching techniques, 56–59
Push-ups, 26–29

Respect, 4, 166
    mutual bow and, 44
Roundhouse kick, 92–95
Roundhouse knee kick, 100–1

Safety, practice and, 122
Scissors throw, from upper block, 196–98
Screaming, 123
Self-confidence, 170
Self-control, 3
Self-defense, 3. *See also* Mental self-defense
    martial arts and, 5
    teaching, 119
    violence and, 180
Self-defense techniques. *See also* Situational
        self-defense techniques
    blocks, 60–69
    elbow strikes, 72–81
    kicks, 82–99
    making fist, 52–55
    physical, 4–5
    practicing, 7, 122
    punch and block combinations, 70–71
    punching, 56–59
    roundhouse knee kick, 100–1
    safety and, 119
Self-development, 3
Self-discipline, 3
Self-esteem, 3
Self-respect, 2, 3, 166
Shoulder throw
    one-arm, 199–201
    one-arm choke to, 191–93
Shouting, 123
Side elbow strike, 76–77
Side falling method, 104–5
Side kick, 86–91
Situational self-defense techniques, 113–14. *See
        also* Self-defense techniques

Stances
    applied, 48–50
    attention, 41–43
    front, 42, 46
    half-and-half, 42, 47
    natural, 42, 45
Standing submission holds, 178–79
Standing up, 6
Strangers, teaching children about, 4
Strength, personal, 6–8
Stretching exercises
    arm, 22–23
    basic, 14–21
    breathe in–breath out, 10–11
    neck, 22–23
    upper-body, 12–13
Submission holds, 176–77
    grounded, 181–82
    standing, 178–79

Television, violence on, 2, 180

Ukemi. *See* Falling methods
Upper blocks, 60–62
    to outer major sweep, 150–57
    to scissors throw, 196–98
Upper elbow strikes, 74–75
Upper-body exercises, 12–13

Violence, 1–2
    children and, 3
    detesting, 6
Warm-up exercises, 9. *See also* Stretching exer-
        cises
Wrist throws
    basic, 120–21, 183–85
    spinning, 186–90

Yelling, 123

About the Authors

Hidy Ochiai

Nationally and internationally renowned martial arts master Hidy Ochiai is the author of *The Essence of Self-Defense* and *The Complete Book of Self-Defense* (published by Contemporary Books), both highly successful books on self-defense as well as on the fundamentals of karate. He has developed an innovative, effective program called EKP (Educational Karate Program), which has been validated by the New York State Education Department. His major concern is the safety and well-being of all children, and EKP teaches the concepts of non-violence, respect, self-discipline, self-confidence, and concentration to students from kindergarten to high school. EKP is taught as an official curriculum by physical education teachers who have been trained and certified by EKP Institute. The students learn basic skills for self-defense, safety awareness, and the fundamental aspects of traditional karate.

Derek Ochiai, MD

Derek Ochiai, MD, is a graduate of Cornell University and Case Western Reserve University Medical School. He is a two-time national karate champion and seven-time All-American. He has been instrumental in teaching and developing self-defense classes for children with Hidy Ochiai. He is a resident doctor in orthopedic surgery at the Albany Medical Center, Albany, New York.